ÁNGELA COVAS RIERA

Never say I wish

*"The loveliest book in the world...
at least for me."*

www.angelacovas.com

Original Title: Ojalá no digas Ojalá.

Proofreading and editing in Spanish by Silvia Díez Mayans

Translated from the Spanish by Christy Cox and Peter Gauld.
I would especially like to thank Maria Angels Puig for her invaluable advice.

Cover by Anónimo Comunicación.

(www.anonimocomunicacion.com)

I love people to write to me telling me what they thought of my book. Don't hesitate even for a second. If you have any comment to make, please do so. You can find me at info@angelacovas.com

For Yram Marrero and all those people who, like him, would rather turn into a fish than give up on themselves.

For Cristina Sarabia, the fairy godmother who with her magic wand makes great things happen to me: like this one, I hope.

ÍNDICE

ABOUT MIRACLES
and opportunities

We all have two lives.
The second one starts when we realize that we
only have one.

Tom Hiddleston

Life is a miracle. A precious gift. A unique opportunity. Both you and I owe our life and our existence to an infinite series of chances. I am here because my father and my mother met at the right moment and decided to share life with each other. They conceived me at the exact moment when I could be born. Out of all those encounters, luckily, they conceived me, Angela, at that specific time, not a day before or a day after. And I was the one who won the race of life, not someone else. Out of the roughly two hundred and fifty million spermatozoa, the one which fertilized the ovum was my other half, my spermatozoon me (sorry, siblings, beat you to it).

I won life. And I had a 0.0000004% chance of doing it. Most probably if I had been told beforehand, I would not even have tried, I would have given up very quickly. But thank heavens, nobody told my spermatozoon part.

My children exist because I met their father on a trip which in spite of everything being against it happening, I ended up making, despite the fact that if I had paid attention to all the signs I would probably never have gone. Or perhaps, without my knowing it, everything came together so I would make the trip, and so that my gaze would meet that of the man who would be my significant other and the father of my children across a beautiful square under a full moon. I might not have started that adventure, or ever met his glance, since there were hundreds of men in that square. But it was his gaze that met mine, and that fact, and every step we took from then on — neither one more nor one less — led us to have exactly the children we have. They might have been different, but all that causality, all the infinite universe behind us, conspired so that things would happen just as they did, and that it was them, our children, not any other combination of an egg of mine and a spermatozoon of their father's.

But before this could happen, my father and my mother too owed their lives to an infinite series of coincidences very like mine. My mother exists because when my grandfather left home to do his military service he passed through my grandmother's village, they saw each other, and spent eight years writing passionate love letters to each other. Luckily nobody else crossed paths with my maternal grandparents during this time, so they got married and at just the right moment conceived my mother, who also won the race between millions of spermatozoa. My paternal grandparents met by chance as well, and so it has always been, forever and ever, since the dawn of time. Your life, my life, are the exact outcome of everything that has happened in the world during the thousands of millions of years our planet has existed.

If we watch the history of the universe from its birth after the Big Bang (if that theory is right), our lives are no more than a brief instant which lasts more or less no time at all. Our time is finite, minuscule, like a tiny molecule of water out of all the water on earth. Yet at the same time we are a miracle, something immensely great, since we barely even had a chance of being born.

Knowing myself to be so big and at the same time so small makes me feel very special, and yet at the same time very free. It makes me feel that if it is so difficult to reach life, I have an obligation to live it as best I can. If my time is finite, I need to take all possible advantage of it. So why have I sometimes been so afraid to live? Why are you afraid of making decisions, knowing perfectly well what you must do and yet being afraid of doing it?

All the books I have published so far, even those I am still writing, are born out of personal experiences from which I have learnt a lot, and I share what they have brought me with my readers. They come from the wisdom I have gathered by falling and getting up again, over and over.

All the books I have written are those I would have liked to have read at some point in my life: books for seeking comfort and wisdom after a breakup, as a teenager, at the start of a project... Each of them is the book I would have liked to have on my bedside table at that particular moment.

This has made me wonder about the kind of book I would like to have on my bedside table today. What is the wisdom I need now but have not yet found? How can I get ahead of myself in order to know what I need right now so as to have my perfect future? Who knows? Who can I ask?

And only one answer came to my mind: I am the only person in the world who has these answers. Not my current *me*, but the person I will be when I go through all the experiences I need to go through in order to learn EVERYTHING I have to learn in my short life.

I am the only one who will know what book I need right now. I am the only one who will have been wrong the right number of times to learn all the things I have come to learn in this world. It will be myself, I hope in a very long time ahead, on my deathbed. The *me* an instant before my life ends, when I barely have a moment left before I leave this body.

No other person will ever have the answers I need, because nobody else will have lived my life, nobody else will know enough about me, nobody else will have walked in my shoes.

And I know that this, the moment I am in right now, just as I will go on to tell you, is the exact moment to have this conversation with my imaginary *me*.

When I think about what that Angela of the future would say to me, I know she would tell me I have a duty to make the most of each second of this miracle that has been granted to me, because she no longer has the time, because if she could, she would: so for me and for her, I know I have to do it.

When my life ends, when I have to cross that door toward death, I, like Saint Peter, will hold myself accountable, and I will want to be sure I have made the most of my time, and that *yes*, that answer, will be my only asset, the most important thing I will carry with me in this life, my entire riches. And if that answer is *no*, then I will feel poor and miserable.

I want to say *yes* with my head high, I want to be able to say I have enjoyed my time intensely, I want to be able to sing Frank Sinatra's *My Way* at the top of my voice, even if it seems a touch extravagant for someone on her death-bed. I want to feel I have lived my life, the one I wanted, not the one others might have decided for me. I want to have made the most of my time and not simply lived through something meaningless.

I know this is the only race I will voluntarily want to win in my life, my best and only achievement, the only one that means anything. And my success will be to have lived according to my principles, enjoying to the fullest what life offered me, learning from my mistakes, bearing the woes as best I could.

Who is this book for?

This book is for everyone, for anybody who wants a full life that makes sense.

But I believe it is particularly a book for me at a time when I need to write it, even to the extent of setting other personal projects aside.

I have always been leaving my comfort zone. Now I have come to a moment when I realize I have fulfilled many of the goals I had set out to reach. When I did my training in coaching, around 2008, I wrote down the things I wanted to achieve on my way through this world. My perfect life was to spend one or two days a week at home, wearing comfortable clothes, sipping my tea, working from home, in peace and quiet. To have a significant other, two children, a house with a garden, to work as a coach, to travel every once in a while — without having to get up early — to be in touch with people I could learn from and who could help me be more aware, good friends to share things with...

Life and my work have given me everything I asked for. Nowadays everything I wrote all those years ago has come true. I work in a field I am passionate about, I have published several books, I live with my other half, the father of my two absolutely special children, and I am surrounded by people who love me. And now that I am here, suddenly I feel strange. I have the life I wished for then, and yet I feel the lack of any major goals.

The feeling of emptiness has been more obvious than that of pride, and this has led me to think that there must be something I need to learn at this point. At this stage of my life I feel I have always been fighting for something or other. First it was for a university degree, later for my work in IT. When at last I achieved that, I fought to get on in my professional life. Then I studied coaching, and then I fought to get my degree in psychology so that I could leave my job and devote myself to living by the things I really liked: coaching, love, writing, sharing... And to these, of course, you have to add other personal challenges such as getting out of unsatisfactory romantic relationships, or having children, or a million other things.

After being used to a life of sailing against wind and tide, weathering storms and hurricanes so as to reach the peaceful haven I find myself in at present, this longed-for peace, this almost dream-like existence seems strange to me, and I feel I need to go in search of something far deeper. It might be the famous mid-life crisis, or as Tom Hiddleston says, perhaps it is the beginning of my second life, the one that starts when I realize I only have one, that this one does not last forever, that this is serious.

That is why this book is for you - if you think you might find it useful ☒ ☒
but most of all it is for myself. It is a process of personal research, a project that appeals to me greatly so that I can learn more about life, and above all to learn more about myself.

Where and when was this book written?

I am starting to write this book in Cuba. This is my first long vacation in three years. Three weeks devoted to myself and my family, three weeks without internet, WhatsApp, email, or any messages from outside in the form of notifications from Facebook, Twitter or email. It has been years since I spent so long in digital silence, so much so that I did not realize it was still possible. And seeing how things work in Cuba, whenever I come back again this digital silence will not be imposed but voluntary.

At this moment the only thing to disturb (or rather add to) my peace and enrich my spirit is my children playing around me, painting, telling me things in the shade of a terrace, while we wait for the hottest hours to pass so we can go out for a walk, to the river or the beach. Three weeks of swimming, of waterfalls, of rivers, of meals with friends, with wonderful people I love to share my time with, with whom there has been a special connection from the very first time we met.

I visited this beautiful green island for the first time ten years ago. At that time neither internet nor electronic communications had entered our lives. Perhaps until today I had never been aware of the implications this has had for us. Ten years ago we lived differently. But during these days I have become aware through my own experience of all the interruptions we have around us. At the moment I am awed at being able to write without wifi, or the beeping of my cell-phone.

Cuba has always seemed a magical place to me. And its people have always surprised me with their wisdom and generosity. Here time goes by differently, the hours seem longer and the days allow far more things to be done than in other places.

Children are the village's communal assets and are revered by its inhabitants. You feel that people love the children and everybody looks after them. If my own go out to play and stray a little too far, all the neighbors, who are outside too, keep an eye on them.

But the gift this island and its people give me every time I come, in a very special way, is a share of their emotional wisdom, their love, their time and their food.

When my vacation began I was determined to finish another book I had begun some time before, but when I sat down at my computer my fingers, my head, my whole being started typing on their own. At first I felt puzzled and said to myself: *Hey! Remember your goals, this isn't what you wanted to do. You're a coach, teach by example, don't lose your focus.*

After a momentary argument with myself I decided to let myself go and forget about the focus. I am on holiday after all, and intuition, the flow, and happiness are an important part of coaching, so I am not straying from my goals. I am simply moving them in time.

Over the days I have become a little more "transcendental". I believe this place, this trip, this moment in my life, coincides with the moment my future *self* has chosen to communicate with me, and that I, my mind filled with thoughts and my fingers transcribing them, am simply the means that future *self* has chosen to leave this message.

My body begs me for this gift in the form of time, words, love, peace, quiet, reflection, digital silence, perhaps so as to reach a commitment with myself to live a life I can be even prouder of. A life well lived.

If you feel like it you can join me on this trip and follow me through this book that is so special to me: a mixture of my holidays, of what Cuba has taught me and of what my *self* tells me on my deathbed. Who knows, you too may learn something. Perhaps this, as well as being my own gift, can be yours.

Real experiences.

I wanted to enrich this book with testimonies from people with a wide perspective of life. For this reason I asked several people three questions.

This was the result.

1) If you could go back to one single day in your life, any day you choose: what would you do that you didn't? Or: what decision would you make that you didn't? Or: What would you *not* do that you did? You will find some of the answers in this book.

2) What's the best decision you've ever made in your life?

In every case the answers to this question were the same. The best decision people usually make is to leave, to say goodbye, to move away from the things that made them unhappy and go in pursuit of their dreams. Some of the answers were: *to be brave, to take risks, to change cities, to change jobs, to say goodbye to people who did not make me happy, to accept my sexuality and live it freely, to leave a marriage that did not make me happy, to change my profession, to fight to study what I really wanted, to have my children...*

After years of professional life, I recognize in this list the things that frighten people the most. It is odd how the things that scare us most end up being the best decisions of our lives.

3) If you could leave just one message and one only, to the child you love the most in this life, or to humanity in the future, what would that message be?

In this case too the answers are similar: *be happy, don't beat about the bush, life is a lot easier than it appears to be, be yourself, there's nobody like you, flow with life, search for happiness in every corner, carpe diem, enjoy every moment, be happy without hurting anybody or letting others hurt you, be honest with other people but above all with yourself, fight for your dreams, share your happiness with people who know how to appreciate it, look for your own understanding of life...* among others.

c h a p t e r   o n e
DEATH

"Pale Death with impartial foot knocks at the
hovels of the poor and the palaces of kings."

Horace

In order to communicate with my future self I need to know more about death. Death is something that has always been around me. I come from country stock, my grandparents farmed and so did my parents. That in itself already connects you to death.

Ever since I was a little girl I have seen hens, and have played with them, but I have also seen how they went into the pot for the stew that would be our meal that day.

I have also witnessed the death of many dogs that have accompanied me through my whole life. One of the best-loved dogs in the history of my family was Olga, a German shepherd whose mother could not look after her, so my mother adopted her when she was two or three days old. She was my tireless playmate, the one who howled beside me as I was learning to walk so that someone would come and pick me up when I fell. The one who listened patiently, moving her head from side to side, when I decided to tell her the story of Little Red Riding Hood over and over, in our own family version (for us, it was always Little Red Riding Hood who ate the wolf). But one day Olga disappeared, she was not there any longer, I was left without my playmate. Something happened, there were tears, sadness, an aura of mystery in which the body disappeared, I guess so that I would not see it. Olga had died.

I have always been very aware of the existence of death, but it is now, probably because I am the right age, a few years past forty, that I am ready to know what death has to teach us. And though at first glance it might seem a gloomy path to follow, knowing more about death leads us to become even more connected with life.

As I do not have access to the internet on this trip I cast an eye over the things I have saved in my computer over time, and at the notes in a notebook where I always jot down things that interest me. Then I realize that this really is the book my fate wants me to write. My notebook opens at the page I needed, one of many I had forgotten I had written. At some point I heard about Bronnie Ware, an Australian girl who had looked after elderly and terminally ill people for many years. During that time she decided to gather together some of the most far-reaching things people say before dying. Bronnie Ware published a post on her blog which went viral, and from there went on to publish her book *The top five regrets of the dying: a life transformed by the dearly departing* (Ware 2013). In her blog she summed up what the people she accompanied in their last moments would have liked to know, or would have liked to change if they had been able to go back in life. There were five points, five *I wishes*:

1)   I wish I'd had the courage to live a life true to myself, not the life others expected of me.

2)   I wish I hadn't worked so hard.

3)   I wish I'd had the courage to express my feelings.

4)   I wish I'd stayed in touch with my friends.

5)   I wish I'd let myself be happier.

I go on looking through what I have so as to have a starting point, and I find a book by Elizabeth Kubler-Ross on my computer: *The Wheel of Life*. This Swiss psychiatrist, who studied the process of death and interviewed many dying people, says that when it is near, it is not frightening. As she explains, people face this last moment one way or another according to how they have lived. You die more peacefully if you feel you have known how to make good use of your life.

I also find Ric Elias, a man who nearly died on Flight 1549 which touched down on the Hudson River in 2009. A flock of birds had crashed against the engines of the plane, which caused a serious mechanical failure. The skill of the pilot, Chesley Sullenberger (another very interesting character), brought the plane down on the Hudson River, saving the lives of all the passengers in the process. But for a few minutes everybody thought they were going to die. Ric Elias, CEO of Red Ventures, talked about what he had learned during those minutes in a TED talk (https://www.ted.com/talks/ric_elias?language=es). He sums it up in these three points:

1)   Your whole life can change in an instant.

2)   I regret the time I wasted on things that didn't matter. I choose to be happy.

3)   Dying isn't scary, but I didn't want to go; I love my life.

But I cannot speak of death and inspiration without recalling what has most likely been one of the most inspiring speeches of the history of mankind. Even though, at the time Steve Jobs was not yet close to dying, he gave a brilliant speech at the University of Stanford. I practically know it by heart. Whenever I have doubts, I can find almost any answer I need in dear old Steve's speech. There are some revealing sentences I always keep in mind, and they are the following:

1)   Sometimes life hits you on the head with a brick. Don't lose faith.

2)   You can't connect the dots looking forward; you can only connect them looking backwards.

3)   The only way to do great work is to love what you do.

4)   If you live every day as if it was your last, someday you'll most certainly be right.

Gaona, the author of *On the other side of the tunnel*, holds that anyone who has been close to death not only loses the fear of dying but loses, at some fundamental level, the fear of living, and that all of them experience deep changes in their scale of values. Some even comment that after such an experience their character has changed.

According to this author, when people become aware of death they usually show the following attitudes:

1)   Asking for forgiveness.

2)   Forgiving.

3)   Expressing gratitude.

4)   Expressing love.

5)   Saying farewell.

I believe all this information is exactly what I need in order to go on with this trip into the depths of life and the mystery of death.

AND WHAT IS
there beyond death?

*"If people knew the nature of death, they'd cease
to be afraid of it. And if they ceased to be afraid
of it, no-one could rob them of their time any
more."*

Michael Ende (Momo)

What will there be beyond death? I must admit I have never been much of a believer. Perhaps I was during my childhood, later to become a convinced atheist, whilst now I might call myself more agnostic than anything else. Meaning that I have sampled all the options. But that is good, because as my friend Juan Carlos Arrese says, something becomes more ethical the more points of view it has experienced. Which means that as far as my beliefs about death are concerned I seem to be following the ethical path.

Many of the authors and specialists who have researched near-death experiences, like Gaona, Kübler-Ross or Brian Weiss, agree that when we die we go through a tunnel of light in which we can revisit our whole life, and in which we feel infinite love. We cease to be mothers, fathers, children, workers, to become the purest essence of our being. The infinite love that fills us mingles with our essence, melting into a whole.

Many scholars of the subject have gathered and interviewed thousands of people who have had NDEs (Near Death Experiences) but who did not die. Many of these tell how they left their own body and were even able to witness what was happening around them. They say they could see their own lifeless body, perhaps on the road after an accident, or on the operating table. Some were even able to visit different places, for example their own home where their spouse or family was busy. Others had stories to tell about things that happened without their being present, causing amazement among people who were there on the spot.

This also chimes in with experiences told me by people close to me who have had an NDE. I did not even have to go in search of them; simply going outside to enjoy the fresh air with neighbors, or sharing anecdotes with friends, I have been able to note how many similar stories there are.

Several religions too hold that we pass through this world changing bodies, going from life to life, learning from each one until we reach freedom through the union with God. This is what we know as Reincarnation.

In Buddhism, for example, the strange *Tibetan Book of the Dead* or *Bardo Thodol* tells how after death, and for a period of forty-nine days, the soul of the deceased passes through different stages, or *Bardos*, as these extra-corporeal states are called, until at last it comes to a great light which it enters to reach perfect unity with the divine (if the soul is ready) or to be born again in another body (if it is not), in which case it retreats before the light.

In India, too, similar ideas are linked to the concept of *karma*. Thus the *dharmic* religions hold that reincarnation is an infinite cycle (the wheel of *karma*) from which we can only free ourselves when our good intentions are sufficient. According to some, we will even be reborn into the form of animals or demons if we have committed sins and evil deeds.

Before the arrival of Christianity, reincarnation used to be a more widespread belief than we might think. In ancient Egypt, life after death and the judgment of the soul before Horus was one of the key aspects of their religion. Pythagoras, who had supposedly traveled to Egypt, introduced to Greece the idea of the transmigration of souls, which became one of the dogmas of the school he founded and which mixed spiritual-religious concepts with scientific knowledge.

Plato also takes up the idea of reincarnation and adapts it to the development of his particular doctrine of Ideas in order to explain how we gain knowledge. According to him, much of what we learn is really a reminiscence of those eternal ideas, or perhaps of previous lives. With the triumph of Christianity all these beliefs were relegated to a lower level and replaced by the concepts of heaven and hell.

After the boom the eastern religions enjoyed with the coming of the 60s counterculture, and in the paradigm of a far more globalized world, the idea of reincarnation has taken on renewed force in spite of the powerful arguments against it. Thus, its detractors ask: where do so many souls come from if there are more and more humans on the planet? and: where were all these souls before mankind ever existed?

Currently, for example, the case of the American psychiatrist Brian Weiss is interesting. When he hypnotized a patient during a session he established that there is indeed a connection to past lives. From then on he continued to research this subject by means of hypnosis and now believes, and strongly defends, the existence of reincarnation. In his view we come to learn something different in each of our lives. It is we ourselves who decide what we want to learn, and with this goal choose our parents and the kind of life we want to live. Through the centuries, and through our successive lives, we sometimes meet the same people. Perhaps your best friend was your child in a past life, or a brother or a sister.

If I were able to believe in anything, I would love to believe in Brian Weiss. I would love to think that my children have chosen me as a mother, that my significant other and I have met in other lives and have come together again in this one, and that in some other life, or perhaps in this one — since I have always been very impatient and the idea of waiting for another life makes me rather restless — I might meet my grandmother Joana Aina, whom I miss so much. I would love to believe that my true friends and I have known each other for infinite centuries, as it sometimes appears, and that we go from life to life searching for each other, so as to have a glass of wine and a good laugh and lend a hand when need be.

I would not even mind being my children's daughter some day, so as to take my small revenge and use up all their felt pens and crayons. On the other hand becoming my mother's mother might be dangerous, because I am quite certain that her sweet revenge would be served cold, the way she has always wanted and never fails to let me know via the roguish twinkle in her eye whenever my children play pranks on me.

But I do not think I really believe. Even though there is nothing I would like more, because if I believed that this is just one life among many, if I believed I would see the people I love again, if I believed I had come to learn, if I believed all this, then I would allow myself to be even freer, and death would become the beginning of another great adventure in which I would play at identifying the people I loved so much in this life.

If I believed, I would feel freer to make mistakes, to enjoy myself, to be happy, to love, to live, because I would not be betting it all on one life. If I made a mistake I would still have a whole universe of infinite lives ahead of me to keep learning, to remedy my mistakes and to be with the people I love. And besides, the love I feel for those around me would be even greater because I would always have loved them, throughout all those other lives, and I would love my children because they had chosen me. I hope they remember that when they are teenagers and start grumbling about their mother as they establish their own identities.

But despite my doubts, in spite of my agnosticism in this matter of reincarnation as well, despite the fact that my scientific mind wants me to hold on to the paradigm of a finite life, I cannot deny that there are many things, not only in the life of others but in my own, which have no explanation in my rational mind.

I have always been someone with good intuition, sometimes even touching on a gift for precognition. How can we explain without magic, without the beyond, with nothing but reductionist science, all those things that happen to me and to so many other people? How can we explain that feeling you and I have sometimes both experienced on meeting someone, that certainty that runs through your body, even more the certainty that runs through your soul, your whole being, that you have always known this person even though it is the first time you have seen them? How can we explain these surges of clairvoyant intuition when we know something is going to happen in the future?

How can we explain the fact that my grandmother appeared to me in my dreams the other night? It was so real... She did not say anything, but she was in the house I live in, which was her own just before she died. She made *burballes*, my favorite dish, without a word to me, but her gaze was more loving than ever. During the whole dream I felt love so intense, so infinite, it is impossible to explain beyond science.

Although I still do not believe in reincarnation, I like to feel as if I did. There are a thousand cases where I do not know what to believe, but I am sure that magic and intuition exist, and that what we are living, this opportunity, is a gift. And I do believe in the tunnel of light at the end, that what remains at the last instant is love. I believe this is the definitive search, the most important one for human beings, and that it is not absolutely necessary to be near death in order to learn the things I need, or to be love.

YOUR WHOLE LIFE
can change in an instant.

"Perhaps sometimes life shows you a side of itself
which leaves you with nothing more to say."

Alessandro Baricco (Silk)

And as I write these words, at the age of 42, I feel I have not yet reached the middle of my life, given that I intend to die at a hundred at least, surrounded by grandchildren and great-grandchildren. None of us, if we are healthy, think anything is going to change in the next few moments, or in the next few days. We take it for granted that everything is going to stay the same, and that following our routine we are going to keep moving ahead on our way. We think about what we are going to eat tomorrow, about those small savings that will allow us to buy this or that, about our holidays, about putting the garden in order or tidying the wardrobe, about the price of oil or what the risk premium is ...Where are we heading to?

We believe that everything will follow in the right order, that we will die as old people before our children do, and before our grandchildren. Our plane will not crash, we will never have an illness that wrecks our health or that of our loved ones, a car will not run us over, or anything like that. Because these things do not happen to us, or our families. Until they happen.

Just in the street where I live, with no more than thirty houses, there are two very young widows. The first one's husband drowned; at a nearby beach a current dragged him out to sea and he did not survive. The other woman's husband, in his early thirties, died of a sudden stroke one night. Last summer a teenage boy slipped away from home one night on his motorbike and never came back. While his parents were looking for him near the house, he was lying dead by the roadside twelve miles from his home. It may be that they, like you and me, thought these things only happened to others.

I am not trying to be a wet blanket, nor to cause fear. What I want is for you to be aware that you can live every day intensely and enjoy this precious gift which is life.

We are not aware that our entire world could change in an instant. This is one of the messages that Ric Elias leaves in his TED talk. The people who went to work in the World Trade Center on 9/11, or those traveling on the train to Madrid on 3/11, or anyone who has had a car accident, or has been diagnosed with a terminal illness… they would never even have imagined it could happen.

Some, as is usually the case in major catastrophes, had a premonition and avoided going. For them too, believing that they knew something bad was going to happen, this must have been an experience which changed their lives forever .

And it all happens in an instant, in a single instant. Before that, life was what it always had been. With the good things and the bad, your tiresome husband or the children who won't leave you in peace, or the next-door neighbor who plays music when you want to relax. With your *I want more, I'm what I am, life is a blast,* or *Life is full of crap.*

Ric Elias, like many of those who have gone through an intense near-death experience, knows there is a "before" and "after". All of them discard the things that are unimportant and spend less time arguing. Knowing life has given them a second chance, that the life they are living now is a borrowed one because it could have ended on that very day, helps them see everything differently. But why do we have to get to that point in order to see life differently?

All your life, all my life, might end the next moment, no matter how much we might believe we have things under control. The truth is that in the blink of an eye we might lose any of those we love most in the world. This state we believe to be perpetual can actually be turned upside down all of a sudden. We have all lost people we loved deeply, and we will go on losing them as long as we are alive.

Being aware of the volatile condition of being makes me give thanks for what I have, makes me appreciate my life, and above all, makes me feel more love for my family.

BUT WHY DO WE NEED
to experience something traumatic to be aware that there is an end?

**"It's so strange how life works. You want
something and you wait and wait and feel like it's
taking forever to come. Then it happens and it's
over and all you want to do is curl back up in that
moment before things changed."**

Lauren Oliver (Delirium)

Many of us are not aware of what we have until we lose it.

My daughter Carmen very nearly died when she was about to be born. The delivery ended in an emergency c-section, which started when only the vertical half of my body was anaesthetized because the epidural did not have the right effect on the other half. A month before my daughter Carmen was born, a couple very close to me, and dearly loved, had lost their first child. A few days before birth his heart failed and he never arrived in this world, with all the sadness that entailed.

When at last I crossed the street from the hospital to my car, with my daughter in my arms and my eyes filled with tears, I felt profoundly thankful to be able to have her, because she was breathing, because she was beautiful, because I was alive, and because my other child, my son Miguel, who at that time was no longer an infant, not yet quite a little boy, was waiting at home.

A few weeks later I had a deep pain in my back that would not let me either lie down or sit leaning on it, I suppose as the result of a c-section which in my gynecologist's own words was the most difficult in her career.

The only position my body allowed me was sitting or standing with my back hunched; any other was intensely painful. There was nothing that could make me comfortable: no pain-killer, no other posture. I could not lie down, I could not sleep, I could not even bathe myself, and my husband had to put my daughter in my arms so that I could breast-feed her. I could not pick up my son Miguel, or do practically anything. I spent four days barely sleeping, because as soon as I relaxed my back muscles the pain became excruciating. On the fourth day I could not stop crying, until my favorite osteopath (as far as I am concerned the best one in the world, Raquel Beltrán) brought me back in the course of a few sessions to being able to live a normal life again.

Since then, and although it was only four days of the most intense pain I have ever experienced, even though I was never anywhere near dying, every morning the first thing I feel when I open my eyes is gratitude for having slept in a bed, for having a body that allows me to hug my children and pick them up in my arms. The pain I had at one particular moment has ensured that my first feeling every day is one of gratitude. Then I look at my children, who end up in my bed most nights, feel their breathing and their warmth in a tangle of intertwined bodies. Then I give thanks a second time.

What happened to me, compared with what many people go through or whatever might happen to me in the future, is trivial. Neither I nor my daughter were in danger, it was not life-threatening, but from that day on it made me focus my attention on the fact that I can lie down and move freely.

And yet before that I had never, ever been so much aware of how important the proper functioning of my body was in allowing me to live a normal life.

But why do we need to lose something in order to be thankful to life, to feel that what we have is a gift, something special, un-repeatable, unique... a miracle? Why do we need a shock like Ric Elias's to appreciate life, to feel the need to be good parents, or never to argue again over silly things? Why do we need to be aware that life is finite in order to choose to be happy instead of stubbornly trying to be right?

Why must something happen before we can lose our fear of living the life we really want? The answer is simple: because, as the people who have been through one of these experiences point out, you realize the greatness of life and the absurdity of fear.

That is what awareness of imminent death brings us: the awareness of life, of its grandeur. That is why those who have been through it agree that they lose the fear of living the life they want. They lose their fear of death because in that experience they are only themselves in the face of the life they are leaving. They stop being fathers, mothers, children, employees or entrepreneurs. They emphasize that when the body separates from themselves only *being* remains, nothing else matters and it is the only thing they take with them, the only important thing. Because of this, when they realize they have been given a second chance they concentrate the remainder of their lives on being that *being*. Must do loses its importance. Everything becomes love, and the chances are that thanks to having been on the brink of dying, they live a second life which is more alive than ever.

WHAT DOES
the certainty
of death bring us?

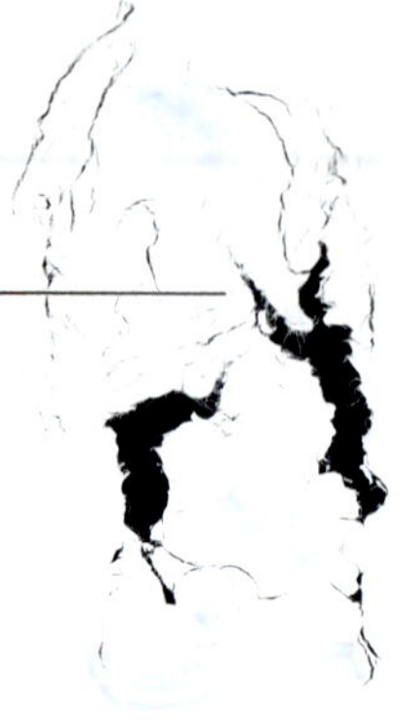

"What you do to escape from her does not matter. Death waits patiently for her moment, hunched behind your shadow, ready to surprise you when you least expect it."

Esther Sanz (The forest of sleeping hearts)

But if you and I already know we are going to die (and we do know it), why do we have to wait until that moment on the border to put into practice all this certainty, this wisdom?

We believe ourselves to be immortal, strong, all-powerful, but we are only a moment in the universe. We know we are going to die, and yet we keep looking the other way, fooling ourselves with trivialities like certainty, routine, or ego. We stay watching the rodeo from behind the fence, cheering yet never venturing out into the open.

Steve Jobs commented in his famous speech that knowing he was going to die was the most important tool he had found for making the great decisions of his life, and I agree. For him this was the greatest proof that he had nothing to lose, for if at the end of the road all that remains is death, he could live more daringly.

The certainty that we are going to die, knowing it, remembering it, knowing that my time, your time, is limited, allows for wise decisions, because the wisest decisions are those that do not know fear, or uncertainties, or being conservative. Knowing I am going to die leads me to think the time I have is limited. The time I have to share with my parents, my children, my significant other, my friends, it is all limited. I no longer have all the time in the world.

IF YOU LIVE EACH DAY
as if it were the last,
one day you will be right.

"Death is angry. It's the moment to put your
tongue out at her."
Jose Saramago (Death with Interruptions)

If you live each day as if it were your last, one day you will be right. This is another of the great quotes Steve Jobs left us in his speech at Stanford. How many *I love yous* unsaid, how many hugs not given, how many kisses, how many *thankyous*, how much forgiveness.

Cuba is so close to me and yet so far. When I am in Spain, it is so close to my heart but so far physically. When I am in Cuba I feel I have always been close, and that I belong to these people and this island.

This is where some of my best friends and my in-laws live. It was four years since I had been here. The decision to concentrate on doing what I most loved had enforced a few economic restrictions on us, among them intercontinental trips.

My other half's mother did not know Carmen, my youngest child. We will be together, the whole family, for a few weeks. Berta, my mother-in-law, has this short period of time to act as a grandmother, until the next time we come. But who knows what might happen before that? I look at her: she acts as a grandmother as if it were the last day of her life, as if she were staking everything on a single card, because she knows that one day she will be right and that her days as a grandmother are fewer than if she lived closer to us.

She spoils my children, makes them all the fruit smoothies they ask her for whatever time of day it may be. She does not scold them and shows a patience I know she does not really possess. She knows that her time is limited and switches on her best version of being a grandmother. Inevitably she has to build, under pressure, a memory of a grandmother which will remain in my children's minds forever. I know how important her grandchildren are for her. Ever since I first met her, even before she knew I would be the mother of some of her grandchildren, she was already proclaiming that the love she feels for her children's children is the most wonderful thing that has ever happened in her life.

When I meet my friends, my brothers and sisters-in-law, I feel as if I had seen them yesterday, as if it had not been four years but just a few weeks. Love is what is present in those hugs; I feel it and so do they.

And as my time here is limited, I too, like Berta, show my best version of myself with my family and friends, and try to be with them as much as I can. We tell each other things, we laugh and enjoy seeing how much the children have grown and how much of each of us is in them.

With them I live these weeks as if they were the last, because I do not know when I will come back and because it will probably be a long time before I do. I look at them and take pleasure in the love I feel for them, and I express it because I do not know what might happen the next time. I live Cuba intensely.

We all live trips intensely because we know they last a limited time, and when they are over we have to go back to our daily life, better or worse, but the everyday one. Life is also a finite journey, with a limited duration.

And it is because of this, because I do not know what might happen tomorrow, that I want to feel the way I feel here now. I want to live day by day being aware that life for me is like Cuba, something so near I can almost touch it with the tips of my fingers and so far that sometimes I forget to live it as it deserves to be lived. This is why I want to live the love I feel for those closest to me intensely and say more *I love yous,* look into their eyes, watch more sunsets and more sunrises, feel that life runs through my veins, have more glasses of wine (or perhaps more cups of tea at my age) with my friends, have more transcendental conversations about the human and the divine.

chapter two

WHAT REALLY MATTERS

"The mystery of human existence lies not in just staying alive, but in finding something to live for."

Fiódor Dostoievski

What a lot of time we waste in absurd arguments, in philosophizing about the past or the present! But how many of these things are really important? How many of them would we do if this were our last day, if we were aware that everything could change in an instant, if we really believed we are going to die, that all this comes to an end, that it is not eternal?

THE EGO

"Pride and the self are two pests of the same family, disguised under the concept of dignity."

Kristel Ralston (Lazos de Cristal)

In his TED talk, Ric Elias muses on those times when (before he believed he was about to die) he had given in to his ego, devoting time to things he did not care about with people he cared about a great deal. As he explains, from that day on and during the two years since his plane crash he has never argued with his wife again.

The word *ego* means *I* in Latin. According to Webster's Dictionary it means *self-importance*. Starting with Freud and the birth of psychoanalysis it has been defined as the conception we have of ourselves, the way we see ourselves, who we think we are. The ego, the personality we believe we have, is built up through our life as a result of our relationship with the external world, the beliefs we come to make our own as we pass from childhood to adolescence and adulthood.

But it is only a vision, the vision of a single person: oneself. There are dozens, perhaps hundreds, of different visions of you. You do not see yourself as your mother sees you, or as your son sees you, or as your best friend sees you, or as the baker you buy bread from every day sees you. If we listen to what our environment tells us about ourselves and little by little make it our own, our vision of the ego becomes richer. This translates into wisdom. And the more wisdom we have, the more we will know how little we know, and the more humble we will be.

If we are not aware of this, if we think only our own construction of reality exists, then we will come to think our own version is "reality", the only one. As in the myth of the cave, in which Plato describes a group of men who have always lived chained up inside a cave, who see the shadows of people passing carrying things and believe this to be the truth. So much so that according to Plato, if one of those men had managed to get out and see reality with his own eyes, then returned to tell his colleagues that they were wrong, they would not have believed him and would have made fun of him.

We can also verify the infinitude of visions of ourselves which build up with the aid of a tool widely used in the business world: *360 Degree Feedback*. Someone's fellow workers, or even his family or friends outside the company, give their opinions about that person's skills and qualities. When the person receives the answers the usual reaction is one of surprise, as the vision he/she has of him/herself does not coincide with that of the others.

But the fewer perspectives we have of ourselves, the more biased the information. It might even happen that even though we have many visions, even though we might know a lot, certain poor, childish egos from our past take over and we behave in a way very far from what is best for us.

The ego likes to be right all the time, not to reveal its weaknesses, to win, and its vision of reality is very limited. As far as it is concerned here are only two versions of things: its own and the wrong one, so that when things do not come out as the ego had decided they should, we tend to grumble and fall into the role of victim.

In these cases the ego looks for culprits when confronted with such situations, and never looks into itself to find them. It does not like to share responsibility for whatever might have happened, preferring others to take the blame. If on top of that (as in my case) the ego is a bit of a chatterbox, then it leads us helplessly to argue with those dearest to us about things that do not matter.

You will be able to recognize your biased vision of reality behind dozens of situations, when you find yourself trying to be right at all costs in an argument, feeling offended when someone expresses an opinion about you or says something you do not like, when you need to come out on top, when you classify the world into winners and losers and feel glad you are in one group, or feel sad about being in the other, when you identify yourself with your successes or your possessions and not with who you really are, when you need to have more and more all the time.

The poverty of our ego is inversely proportional to our happiness. The poorer our ego, the emptier our life. The emptier our life, the more we need our ego to reappear so as to bring us some degree of dignity.

The wounded ego

Poverty deprives the ego of the air it needs to breathe. Without air the ego is wounded, it feels that it is denied existence, and its instinct for survival appears in the form of a deep anger against the world. We can recognize the empty lives around us, people looking to start ridiculous arguments that allow them to reaffirm themselves, to say *I'm here* through ridiculous methods.

Like the man who yells at the traffic lights, or who starts stupid races on the road, or the woman who keeps her place in line at the baker's at all costs.

Or those people who are endlessly worried about what you are doing with your life, ready to criticize anything. I usually keep a little apart from the conventional codes of the society I live in, and yet I have been the frequent object of these criticisms. Who you go out with, where you come from, where you park, what time you serve supper to your kids, what clothes you are wearing...

Many take part in the game and start arguing with the man who shouts at the traffic lights, or criticize someone who has already started criticizing. It is easy to get caught up in the game, but we need to avoid it, because behind all this there is only fear, fear of looking into life itself. People with fear know that the moment they glimpse their own reality the pain will be unbearable, because nothing hurts more than an empty life, and in order to stop it hurting so much, the easiest thing to do is fight against others, not on one's own behalf.

I do not usually join this game, because I have been an expert in fear, because I have suffered it in my own flesh. I know that behind a poor wounded ego, behind envy and meaningless competition, behind that touchiness, are to be found fear, sadness, unhappiness and dissatisfaction.

Life beyond the ego.

The impoverished ego has only a single perspective, whereas the rich ego has many more. Life beyond the poor ego involves playing at trying on different hats and seeing what we think with one or the other on our head.

Dissociating ourselves from our feelings, seeing things from different perspectives without the infinite cloud of socially accepted codes, could help us experience other ways of seeing life.

We can look for those other perspectives in ourselves, or in the situations we find ourselves in, or in other people, but it is not always necessary. You can do it yourself. You just have to raise your eyes and gaze at everything around you, play a little and enrich yourself with the infinite gazes you may find around you.

Many of the people who make the best choices, the fairest ones, know how to play at this. For example, there is a story that the fascinating Israeli Prime Minister Golda Meir, who was known in her time for (among other things) her impressive common sense, used to say that every time she had to make a tough decision she would ask her great-great-grandfather and her great-great-grandson. This gave her a detached view which at the same time was linked with both her roots and with the future.

But you do not need to be a minister, or to go so far, if you do not want to. Just raise your gaze a little. I could give thousands of examples: how would you see life if you were a spectator of your own movie? Or if you were a bird? Or a fish? What does whatever you are going through look like when seen from that star up there? Or from that cloud? Or from a tree a hundred years old? How does the cactus on your table see it? How would Plato see it? What advice would Golda Meir give you? Or Steve Jobs? How would you look at that situation if you were your own son? Or your father, or your mother?

But that still leaves someone even more special you can ask. The person who has all the answers you need, the wisest one for you because she knows you better than anyone else. Although you will have to call upon your imagination, since this person is not here right now, and you will have to travel to other times of your life. What would the child you once were tell you? What would the old man you will be one day tell you? What would your twenty-year-old self say, that young person with hundreds of worlds still to explore? Even more, what would your *you* tell you if you had not been born where you were? And if you had been born into another family, what would that *you* be like?

I usually go back to questions like: what would the teenager who dreamed about a perfect family say if she saw me yelling at my children? Or the mother who has just found out she is pregnant, the one who dropped her new cell phone inside the toilet from the excitement and expectation she felt at the precise moment she knew a life was growing inside her? Or the future mom, the one who is saying goodbye to her children from the front door while they are leaving to live somewhere else forever, if she saw me choosing to watch TV instead of playing with them? What would dying Angela say if she saw me getting bored today, instead of draping life over my shoulder like a cape?

Because in my world I do not have perspective; whereas they, all the others, do. And they enrich my ego, they allow me to fill my lungs with air and see life from their points of view, which are always better than the one which is in the heart of things, the one which cannot see the forest for the trees. The one lost in a sea of feelings which have nothing to do with reality, but which at the same time are more reality than ever.

The grandfather

Marisa's grandfather Josué was ninety when he breathed his last. Marisa had never understood Josué; to her he had always seemed a very strange person. He was jealous, distrustful, bad-tempered. Almost any situation in the world seemed a threat to him, and he spent his life distrustful of everything and everyone. With the exceptions of his daughter, his son-in-law and his granddaughter he threw everybody out of his home, (relatives or not) who were friendly towards his wife, who was known for her kindness, understanding and warmth. He only knew one way of loving, which was possession, and to be at peace he had to keep everyone around him under his yoke. He tried by all possible means to stop his daughter, Marisa's mother, from working or carving out a future of her own; even so, he could not prevent it and Marisa's mother managed to study.

When Marisa asked her family, trying to understand why her grandfather was like that, she found that Josué's mother had brought him up with the stick, probably because it was the only language she knew, and that Josué had worked at home from the age of six. He had not been able to go to school, his childhood was a bad dream he was forced to live through, and he had never ever been able to enjoy his own children. In a very poor family where *save yourself if you can* was the rule, Josué had grown up with no trace of love, compassion, security or joy.

Many people experience this; some evolve and manage to take the side of love and generosity, while others never manage to conquer the dragon of misery they have grown up in and remain trapped in tyranny. Marisa knew this. She was forty, she had lived through a lot in a whole string of countries, had known many people and was a profoundly understanding person. As a result, when Marisa looked at him she felt pity instead of the fear her grandmother and her mother felt.

Josué doted on his granddaughter. He had always given her everything he could. He let himself love her freely, very unlike the tyranny he exerted over his own daughter. And Marisa loved him in her own way.

After living a life full of adventure and professional challenges, Marisa felt it was time to become a mother; and as she had not found a suitable partner to share her life with, she decided to opt for assisted motherhood and a sperm bank and became pregnant.

Inexplicably for her, when she told her grandfather he threw a tantrum and spoke appalling words no pregnant, hopeful woman should ever have to hear. From that moment she never went back to her grandfather's house, until her mother begged her to go as he was prostrate in bed and did not have much time left.

Her grandfather could no longer speak and merely gazed at her sadly. Marisa looked at him indifferently, without any memory of the love she had felt for him and without his death mattering in the least to her. Josué died two days later and Marisa even felt liberated. She decided not to shed a single tear or utter a single farewell. As far as she was concerned her grandfather had died the day he spoke those words. At that moment all the weak pillars their relationship had been based on collapsed, and all the kisses, the memories, the dolls, the presents and the laughter were buried under the ruins.

I met Marisa several years later, when she was working on another of her life projects. At that time she was happy with her daughter and very far removed from the pain Josué's words had caused her that day. That distance allowed her to see the situation from afar, to interpret it anew and attach different meanings to it.

Marisa learnt many years later that her grandfather's words had hurt her ego and made her forget the years they had spent together. This led her to admit that her last glance at her grandfather had been one of hatred mingled with indifference, instead of one of understanding of an unhappy childhood and a life devoid of enriching experiences. She had stooped to his level instead of being above all that sort of thing. And now that she had forgiven him, deep down she wished him to rest in peace, and she would have liked to exchange her last gaze, one of indifference, for a whisper in his ear: *farewell.*

THE BATTLES
that really matter

*"We live in the era of secrecy and fear. You must
have two faces. Show one to the crowd and
keep the other for yourself and your creator. If
you want to keep your eyes, your ears and your
tongue, forget you have them."*

Amin Maalouf (Samarcanda)

The battles that really matter are sometimes those we fight the least. Those that do not matter, which are often the very ones we choose, are the tree that stops us seeing the forest, the ones that keep us frustrated and take us away from the things that matter.

I have battles that truly matter still to be fought in my life. I feel that I bow in submission in the face of things that are essential. Perhaps I ought to fight harder for the education I know my children, and many others, should have. It is a battle that truly matters, but I do not fight it strongly enough. Maybe not even my own share.

There are also battles which are much less titanic, like solving that nuisance that bothers us every time that... For some, it happens every time they go into their workplace, for others every time they get into bed with their other half, others again when they open their eyes each morning...

And then there are still smaller battles, which nevertheless are usually the biggest: the melancholy we feel when we realize how long it is since we had a good laugh, or when we are surprised by something, or when we have not spent a while doing something we genuinely love.

These are the battles which provide a mask for our poor ego, the ones that stop us from looking in the mirror, from feeling compassion for ourselves, or being brave, walking away, closing doors, laughing at everything, but particularly at ourselves. These are the battles we do not confront.

On the other hand we devote time on battles that are unimportant and could be solved ridiculously simply, as for example when we argue with our significant other about how to fold the dishtowels, or which way the shower curtain should go. Or with our children, about whether they have to wear this or that, or finish their food, or eat certain things.

We spend a great deal of our life fighting for things that do not matter in order not to have to pay attention to the ones that really do, the ones that could enable us to live a life well lived, not to be saying *I wish...* when we find ourselves at death's door.

FORGIVENESS

"Life is not what one lived, but what one remembers and how one remembers it in order to recount it."

Gabriel Garcia Marquez (Living to tell the tale)

According to Gaona (2014), asking for forgiveness and forgiving are two of the five things or attitudes he has detected in people who realize they are near the end of their life.

When a painful event has occurred between two or more people, if there has been no forgiveness, if the wound is still open, there will continue to be a barrier of resentment, sadness or emotional pain in both directions.

Forgiving

"It is never too late to have a happy childhood."

Milton Erickson.

Some people say that forgiveness comes when you admit there was never anything to forgive, simply that there might have been something which needed to be understood. I feel that this phrase has its limitations, because there are times when understanding might not be within reach.

For me, forgiveness arrives when you realize that whatever happened, whatever someone did to you, was not important enough for you to hold a grudge in your heart. When you realize that as long as you bear a grudge you are not free, when you become aware that somewhere in your body there is a flame burning that stops you living a full life and being yourself.

When we do not forgive, several attitudes come into play, among them that of the victim: the guilt I am feeling belongs to the other and there is nothing I can do about it. I am hurt because of that other person's decision. Bear in mind that in that case you are handing over all the power of your emotions to the other person, and the one who hurt you once still has the power to do it every time you think about it.

Within this attitude we can distinguish various subdivisions.

Conditions. If the other person asks for forgiveness, if the other person shows me this or that, then I will be able to forgive him/her. In this case we go on building up resentment in our heart as we wait for the other person's action. We keep handing power to the other person, waiting for them to *"do something"* we have decided they must. This is curious, because very often we have not even told the other person what they have to do, or what we expect them to do.

Revenge. In this case we hope to inflict pain similar to what we received, or are going through, ourselves. This is a double-edged tool, because it could end up as war.

To go deeply into the subject of forgiveness is a difficult task which would probably require a whole book in itself, and is not the object of this one.

But what happens when there is no more time left? What happens when you have no more time to negotiate? To plan revenge? Perhaps when you have the choice there in front of you, the choice between resentment and forgiveness, you will choose love. This might give support to those who claim that after we die we become an entity which is only love. Why not? It is possible because, among other things, as there is no longer a future we opt for love instead of resentment.

And the fact is that feeling oneself to be the object of an offense, building up resentment, is very much connected with the ego, and also to the battles that really matter. Because if in this precise instant when you are reading these words you choose resentment, you are choosing to fight a battle which will cause your life to move ever further away from you, a life possessed by the pain someone caused you in the past. And does that battle really matter? Are you really choosing to waste your time, your thoughts, on something you cannot change? True, you cannot erase it from your past, but you can erase it from your future, you can make sure it does not take up residence in your life, or write your script for you.

But I have to tell you that the past is nothing more than a story you tell yourself, in which you have created your own truth. You might choose to tell yourself other different versions and they too would be true. So that in order to forgive, you yourself can choose the story you want: some will make you walk forever with a dark cloud in your heart; others, on the other hand, will make you feel freer to fly even higher.

What is curious is that very often we keep the worst version for ourselves, the one that hurts us most, the one that makes us behave as rigidly as possible: being sad, angry, wanting to be right, the "right" of the impoverished ego.

Flexibility - towards yourself as much as to others - is one of the keys to happiness, and if you believe that only your own truth is real, that there is no room whatsoever for any other, then you are losing the magic of infinite truths which will make you free, and which you have yet to discover.

And now you know that, what is the sense of choosing the most painful truth?

It is in your own hands; only you have that power.

Forgiving oneself

It has always been easier for me to forgive others. Perhaps this was instilled in my mind thanks to my past at a Catholic school. Perhaps because I have always been good at empathy and have been able to put myself in somebody else's shoes and understand them. Or perhaps I have simply not wanted to waste time on things that were unimportant, or that hurt me. I do not know.

What I do find difficult, though, is to forgive myself. I have the unhealthy habit of going over and over some of the decisions I have made in the past: what if I had studied what I really wanted to when I was eighteen? And if I had not chosen to share my life with those people at that moment? And not wasted time? And made use of my time? What if...?

And although I know the theory, I usually end up in the same rut. I know I am what I am on the basis of all the decisions I have made in my life, right or wrong. We are what we are because of the conjunction of the good moments and the bad ones, the failures, the good experiences, the not-so-good ones, the loves and the not-loves. Each and every one of the moments we live define what we are.

Not a single one of my books would have come out of me if I had not been through pain at some point, if I had not lived. If I had always been right, if everything had been perfect, if I had always made the right choice, I would not be the person I am, the friend, the mother, the daughter I am.

And when I decide to focus on it like this I feel big, lucky and free. Whereas when I think about all that I would change, I feel small.

Just as some people I have met decide never to fall in love so as to avoid suffering, so others decide not to live, not to move, not to make decisions, so as to avoid making a mistake. The culture I have grown up in has taught me to value mistakes negatively, so that many people decide not to live to avoid feeling the pain of making a mistake.

There is no way to live without experiences. Without them, we are denying ourselves all the learning they can bring us. Luckily we are seeing the case being made more and more in schools for learning through experience, and the best we can do for our children is to teach them to learn from what might be considered failures.

My friend Javier Pérez told me once that when his son Xabier was very small, on a trip out one afternoon they began to throw pebbles into the water. The little boy threw pebbles but his hands were so small he could not make them fall in the water. Whenever he missed, his father celebrated, clapped, cheered and told him: "You nearly did it, nearly!" Xabier is now six, and when he cannot do something, he tries over and over, and every time he fails he looks at his father with a smile and says excitedly, "Nearly, daddy, I nearly did it!" What a great lesson to have learned, that nearly! And how easy, and at the same time difficult, it is to provide it.

Just as I cannot conceive of life without love, I cannot conceive of it either without living it, without taking risks, without making decisions. And just as in love, to live life without suffering means not to move on, and I would never walk that path. I support Javier's principle of "nearly": "*I might not have everything I wanted, but I have nearly all of it,*" and so with all the "nearlys" that are necessary. So from this moment, when I find myself gazing out at the horizon and the sun going down between the mountains, I choose to turn all my failures, all my blame, all my "what ifs..." into "nearlys", which are what have brought me here to write to myself during this endless vacation. I choose to be glad about all of them, to welcome them into my life, to be grateful for them. And that way there will be nothing to forgive.

Asking for forgiveness

Asking for forgiveness is another thing people find they need when they are nearing their end. Perhaps this is where the sacrament of the Last Rites comes from, so important in the Catholic religion, whose aim is to bring peace for the journey to the other life, and which includes confession and forgiveness of the sins the person feels he/she might have committed.

This need has proven itself to be very relevant since the dawn of time, given that a specific sacrament was created for it.

And knowing we have acted in a way that is not in keeping with our values, or that we have hurt somebody, is a heavy weight on our heart. It usually happens that we are the only ones who carry this weight, while the other person is not even aware of the pain it causes us.

To ask for forgiveness is to tell the other person, the one you have hurt, that you wish you had not done whatever it was that you did, that you too are sorry, and feel the pain of it. And in the end the suffering of both those involved puts people on the same level, brings them closer rather than driving them apart.

And saying "I'm sorry", without waiting to be near the end, also makes us freer and makes our passage through life lighter. We leave the ego behind in order to bow our head and say that what we have done was hurtful to someone else.

"You are my son"

"If I could go back and change just one day of my life, it would be the day I got angry with my son Daniel about his appearance. I have four children, and none of them have turned out the way I expected. But now I see them all grown up, they're all happy in their own way, even though it's not ways I'd have liked. It's cost me a lot to accept this, to accept that the children weren't my own property. It's only now I'm getting older that I can look at it with some detachment.

"Daniel is my youngest. He's a social worker, a responsible young man who does his job well. He's always studying, and he's always paid for those studies himself. Since he was very young he's worked over the weekends as a waiter so as to manage it.

"I'm a traditional sort of man and I like normal people. And I'd have liked my children to be normal too, the way I saw it. I liked serious, well-dressed young men, without earrings and with short hair. Even now I prefer them that way, I can't deny it.

"And Daniel came home one day with horrible dreadlocks. He looked like Bob, the supporting character from The Simpsons. His head was huge, disproportionate. Up till that moment there'd been small changes, not just in him but in all my children, who turned out a bit hippy-ish. An earring here, a piercing there, those horrible wide pants.

"But on the day of the dreadlocks, I got really mad and said horrible things to Daniel, things that are deeply painful for me now that time's gone by. I told him I was ashamed of him and that from that moment he wasn't my son any more.

"*Daniel was furious and stopped talking to me for months. I couldn't understand why he was angry when I was the one who ought to be upset. I mean, he comes home looking like that and he's the one who's offended?*

"*Now, much later, it troubles me that I said those things to him, but what's more painful for me is what happened next. Daniel and I have never gone back to the relationship we used to have. This divided things into a before and an after. Since then, and even though this happened many years ago, we just keep on polite terms. Nothing more than that.*

"*If I could go back I'd change that day and not say anything. At my age, at this moment in my life, I'd give anything to feel he was closer, to know him better, to have him tell me more things than he does.*

"*No, I don't know how to ask his forgiveness, and even if I did I don't think it would change anything. I don't know, perhaps one of these days.*"

Julián, 72 .

ATTACHMENT

*"Yes, brothers, let us thank God for having
made us this gift of death, so that life is to have
meaning; of night, that day is to have meaning;
silence, that speech is to have meaning; illness,
that health is to have meaning; war, that peace
is to have meaning. Let us give thanks to Him for
having given us weariness and pain, so that rest
and joy are to have meaning. Let us give thanks
to Him, whose wisdom is infinite."*

Amin Maalouf (Leo Africanus)

When I was a teenager I did not want anybody to touch my things. I treasured my toys, my teddy bears, my notebooks, as treasured possessions. My sister and my little cousins' favorite game was to play with my soft toys behind my back. They hid when they did it. Like everything, it is a question of contrasts; to have experienced the deepest attachment for a while has let me, over time, travel to the other side, to that of detachment.

After my teenage years my period of upheaval began. During my college years I lived in three different apartments, then went to live with my boyfriend, and after a few years left everything to go and live in London with just what would fit in a single suitcase. Afterwards I spent time in Madrid, living in several houses, and came back to Mallorca a few years ago.

All that moving, that business of starting from scratch over and over, allowed me to experience the other side: having nothing, not being able to take anything with me, and I realized that even so, I did not care. Quite the opposite: having nothing, having left everything behind, made me feel free.

Then, with my children, came detachment from material things, from objects. Their inquisitive, mischievous hands have fallen on practically everything I still had left. Now I no longer have felt pens that write, or lunch boxes with matching lids. The soft toys I saved with great effort from the ruthless claws of my sister and my cousins, a white poodle and the gorilla Monkey-Monkey, drag their innards across the floor of my parent's house in my children's hands, while my cousins (all of them over 30) tell me off because my children can play with Monkey-Monkey and they could not.

My children have put an end to my last feelings of attachment.

I think that now I can travel anywhere in the world with the three pots my grandmother gave me, not so much for their value as because with them I feel her close to me. Everything else is replaceable. I do not care for the jewels I have owned, or the sheets, or the household appliances, or anything of the sort. I could even live without the pots if things got too bad.

When I look around me I realize how much suffering is caused by attachment. Particularly in cases of divorce and inheritance, where attachment to material things, houses, land, objects, cause people to lose sight of who they really are.

They pour out the pain they feel for their losses and feelings of insecurity. When it comes to inheritances many people invest the love their parents denied them as children on their possessions, feeling that if they keep those, the inner emptiness they feel will disappear forever. Afterwards the families are left broken, each member trailing his or her own emptiness.

They stake their identity on the possessions they feel they ought to have. These people value themselves by what they have or what they make. Attachment leads us to believe that without it we will not be happy, or even that we simply will *not be* anything.

I like to experience detachment; it leads me to freedom, it leads me to know that I am me, with or without possessions, it gives me the flexibility to make the decisions I need to make at any moment. I come from a long line of farmers, where arguments about land and fields have always been part of life. And looking at it from a distance, I see those who are now "six feet under" and who disputed over those lands. None of them took it as far as the grave. But on the other hand they wasted a great deal of their life litigating and living in a perpetual state of being upset, instead of gazing at sunsets and enjoying that precious time they no longer have.

Attachment limits us when it comes to making decisions. If you are attached to a possession you will never be able to open your eyes to see better things. Or simply to see. To discover the importance that has, or does not have, in your life.

A dear friend whose job involves constant disputes about inheritances and divorces told me how elderly people would have terrible fights over land and houses, attaching so much importance not to whether they finally got the inheritance themselves but to preventing it from falling into anyone else's hands. Objects ended up obscuring everything else: the love you felt for your brother, the times you crept to his bed because you were afraid, or the times you cried on his shoulder over a broken heart or a punishment. And the same thing happens with people in the throes of divorce, because what was there when they first fell in love, that true magic, is forgotten.

We also experience attachment to significant others and friends. When we are attached to our other half, when we need to know he is there, when we consider this person as *ours*, we also lose perspective. Attachment to the other half is the seed that makes jealousy grow, the thing that makes us believe a person belongs to us, when in fact nobody owns anybody else. Not even our own children belong to us.

I worked for many years in a large company, and could see attachment shining out everywhere. I saw men in suits fighting over a parking space, or an office, or a work project, or a position... things which at the end of our life will have no importance whatsoever. They fight for those things in the same way that brothers have always fought over land.

When I die, I will not be able to take even my grandmother's pots with me. The only thing that will remain of me will live on in my children's memory, and my grandchildren's if I am lucky. Of the pots, only the flavor of their stews will remain, the times they were tasted with a wooden spoon, and the fact that they, and I, cooked together. The experience we had with the pots will remain. Nothing more. What remains of us is not a question of possessions, but only of the time spent together.

The diamond

The sanyasi had arrived on the outskirts of the village and camped under a tree for the night. Suddenly a man from the village ran up to him and said: "The stone! Give me the precious stone!" The sanyasi asked: "What stone?" "The other night," the villager said, "Lord Shiva appeared to me in a dream and assured me that if I came to the outskirts of the village at sundown, I would find a sanyasi who would give me a precious stone that would make me rich forever." The sanyasi searched in his satchel and brought out a stone. "He probably meant this one," he said, and gave it to the villager. "I found it on a path in the forest six days or so ago. Of course you may have it." The man looked at the stone in awe. It was a diamond! Perhaps the biggest diamond in the world, for it was as big as a man's hand. He took the diamond and went home. He spent the night tossing and turning in bed, completely unable to sleep. The following day, at dawn, he went to wake the sanyasi, and said to him: "Give me the richness that allows you to give this diamond away so easily."

Anthony de Mello

THE TIME I WASTED
on things that didn't matter

"Mom knew how to be gay. Mom knew how to be fearful. Mom knew how to forget easily. And yet she had a very good memory. Mom shut the door in my face, but she let me into her bath. I sometimes lost Mom, but her instinct always found me. When I broke glasses, Mom put on the putty. She sometimes sat in error, although there were plenty of chairs around her. Even when she closed up, she was always open for me. She was afraid of drafts and yet she never stopped stirring up winds. She spent, and didn't like to pay taxes. I was the reverse of her medal. When Mom played hearts she always won."

Günter Grass (The tin drum).

According to Ric Elias, this was one of his regrets: the time he had wasted on things that did not matter. Sometimes when I am coaching a group I use something my friend Jordi Llonch taught me. I ask the people to write down on separate pieces of paper five things they want in their lives that are important, whether or not they have them already. They can be material, like a car or a trip, or their family, or their work: whatever they want to write down, bearing in mind that it is a game. Then I make them imagine that whatever they have written down is something they will have, that the game ensures this, and they will be able to live their life with it.

Then I get them to imagine that we are on a plane and that (as with Ric Elias) the engines break down and a genie appears. The genie tells them they will be saved if they let go of one of the pieces of paper, bearing in mind that their life will be saved, but that from that moment they will have to give up what they had written on that piece of paper. We go on with our journey and encounter some cannibals who put us in their pot, and to save themselves they have to give up another piece of paper. And so on until they are left with just one piece of paper.

In the end what is surprising is that the first thing they give up is the thing they normally spend most time on: work, money, or luxuries which become superfluous when you have to choose at some decisive moment. People are left with family, or devotion to a particular passion, or a hobby. If they have children this is usually the piece of paper they are left holding. It is the most valued part of their life.

But we are not aware of this, and invest minutes, days, months and years of our precious time on things that are not really important.

chapter three

A LIFE TRUE TO ONESELF

"I once won a bolero singing competition," she would say, as she sang "Noche de Ronda" in the kitchen. And all of a sudden she broke off the song and turned thoughtful, as if she were imagining that other possible life one always loses in order to live one's own."

Elvira Lindo (Lo que me queda por vivir)

According to Bronnie Ware, this is another of the things people regret at the end of their days: not living a life which is true to oneself, not living the life we want, but instead the one others expect of us, the one others have drawn or sketched out in some way.

We are all born into a family, a society, a village, a country. We are born into the lap of a certain culture, different from one country to another, and in each one of us various subtle differences come together. Subtle differences in existence itself, in religion, in the country, differences inherited from our own family, differences in beliefs, values, in how to see life, of how to design our future. Differences which depend on whether we are the eldest, the youngest or the middle brother. Differences in the economic circumstances our family may have lived through and that we are now living through ourselves.

Subtle differences linked to the fairy-tales of our childhood, the movies we watch, the news we follow, what our friends say, how they see us, what is in fashion, what we perceive ourselves to be, what others show us that they see in us.

Subtle differences in our emotional inheritance, but perhaps in our material inheritance too, the thing our parents expect us to look after. Or perhaps in our duty, the duty we feel to look after those closest to us and which makes us think we are not free.

And at times it is thinking we are not free, believing we are not free, that keeps us anchored to a life that is not ours, which is not the one our heart, our soul, advises.

To enjoy the gift life offers requires us to live a life true to ourselves. To follow our own way, the one we really want, whether or not it is what society wants of us.

Sometimes this makes things difficult, as choosing our own path is almost certain to mean overcoming certain social barriers. Living a life true to oneself is not easy - it requires a great deal of effort - but living the life others have decided that we should live involves a great deal of frustration and resignation.

WHEN THE CAPTAIN
gives an order,
the sailor does not question it

"Apart from that, he was one of those men who
prefer to be present in their own life and consider
it wrong to have any ambition to live it."

Alessandro Baricco (Silk)

If life has taught me anything, it is that where the heart is in charge, the head is not. As the saying goes: *When the captain gives an order, the sailor does not question it.* However much the rational brain may tell us everything is fine, our emotional brain, which is connected to the purest essence of the human being, sends signals that something is going wrong. It is like a ship steered by a sailor who follows the lessons he has learnt in order to guide it to port safely. But it is the captain who really knows where to go. When communication fails between captain and sailor, the ship does not sail smoothly along the waters of life, it is not a happy ship. Of course from the outside it is obviously a ship, but inside it a tension can be felt, caused by the uncertainty of choosing one course or another. And it keeps changing over and over again, making the journey still more difficult.

However much you may reason that your life is the way you would like it to be, that the person you are with is the one who suits you, that your job is perfect, that you are in the right place at the right moment... still, when the heart rebels, when it starts sending signals that something is not right, by now there is nothing to be done.

I find it easy to see it from the outside, still more so with years of experience, with the hundreds of clients I have had the immense pleasure of working with. But even so, sometimes one of the captain's orders eludes me and I go on with my life like a sailor. Time has taught me to detect this, but every once in a while I still get unexpected surprises. Everyone feels it in a different way: some feel a lump in their throat, others a knot in their stomach, others perhaps a weight in their insides.

In my case, there is a dream that recurs again and again when I am living some version of my life I do not like: I can fly. Now, after all the experience I have amassed, I know that when I have that dream it is a sign for me to start thinking about what new place in my life I want to explore.

But usually people do not spend as much time looking into themselves as I do after spending the last decade learning more about personal development and psychology. Many of my clients come to me troubled, torn between the sailor on the one hand, who tells them the life they have is good, and on the other hand the captain, who feels sad, or trapped, or defrauded, or says he has not enough air to breathe. There are as many ways of expressing it as people living in the world.

They have the perfect other half, the best parent for their children or the ideal job, positions of responsibility; perhaps they travel all over the world, or have the perfect parents, or the perfect children. And yet they look around and ask themselves: *If everything's fine, if I can't see what's wrong, if everything's in the right place, why do I feel like this?* They turn to the brain in search of answers, because that is what we have been taught to do. *Think, use your head, go over it, emotions are no use, make a list of the positive aspects.* But the rational mind only has a small percentage of the answers and explanations for our behavior. The experts normally put it between 5 and 7%.

That is why when we sense the alarm signal, when we sense that the captain is whispering, or whining, or even shouting, it is time to ask ourselves all the questions we need to ask. Time to open our eyes and listen in silence, so as to be able to make contact with that call of the earth, of the soul, of the heavens, or wherever it might be coming from, which will enable the captain and the sailor to sail in the same direction.

WHAT WOULD YOU DO
if you were
the last person in the world?

"Teccam has already said it: there is no brave man who has never walked a hundred miles. If you want to know the truth of who you are, walk until not a person knows your name. Travel is the great leveler, the great teacher, bitter as medicine, crueler than mirror-glass. A long stretch of road will teach you more about yourself than a hundred years of quiet introspection."

Patrick Rothfuss (The wise man's fear)

What would you do if nobody cared about what you really wanted to do? If nobody judged you? If you had no fear of the future? If you had no responsibilities? If you really listened to your heart? If you were a millionaire and you had all the money in the world?

Leave your job, perhaps? Do something different? Leave your spouse? Or your country? Or your city? Would you move house? Or would you rather write a book? Or spend more time on art? Plant zucchini? I have no idea. What is your own answer?

Ask the captain, close your eyes and get in touch with your own self, with your true *you*, with your most intimate desires, with your deepest dreams.

That is where you will find the answer to your deepest yearnings. And when you have it, you will feel it was obvious, that that is exactly what it was, that you would never have realized it and yet it was there. And do not fool yourself, responsibilities are a choice. If you are here, if you do not move, it is not because you have no choice in the matter.

Nothing stops you from getting up and leaving. Nobody stops you from leaving it all behind, whatever you happen to be doing. Do not use your children as an excuse because they never asked you to make the sacrifice you are making. You are the one who has decided to stay and do "what you have to do". But consider also: sometimes the best example to give your children is to search for your own happiness, because otherwise you are just teaching them what you learnt yourself: that life is a constant sacrifice, that it is a path of pain and suffering and that it is not possible to have a better life.

Learning to dream

My children have made me freer to make decisions because I know that my duty is to teach them how free people act. Because just as previously you might find parents who wanted their children to be lawyers because that was what they would have liked to do themselves and lacked courage, or were unable to, so we now find parents who want their children to be what they really want to be, because they themselves were unable to.

And these parents feel lost when confronted by their children's frequent lack of interest. They cannot understand why they, who have the opportunity, do nothing, do not choose, do not study and instead spend their time on the couch. I work with teenagers on a project called VadeVida (*It's all about life*). We have a special program for them called "Somiatrui-tes" (*Dreaming about omelets,* or *"castles in the air"*), which lasts about a week.

The first thing we teach them is something they do not know how to do, unlikely though it may sound: to dream. Dreaming requires its own methodology. Dreaming is not about seeing the paths in front of us and deciding which one to choose. Dreaming consists of imagining a place to go to and then finding the way. Because if we only see the ways ahead of us, our destinations are very limited. If a lad only sees that he has college ahead of him, and that once there he can choose between law, medicine or engineering, he will miss so many other things.

Another condition for dreaming is that it is not necessary for the place to exist for us to imagine it. I always use food as a metaphor. You do not need to imagine you want to eat a paella in order to start dreaming, rather than that you sometimes have to begin with the ingredients. Perhaps we start out thinking we fancy a dish with shrimp and mushrooms. This leads us not only to paella but to many other places: a dish of pasta, crepes, garlic shrimp with mushrooms, or noodles, and this is just to begin with. And starting from there you can be more precise and search for paths.

When I work with young people I find that their dreams are not down-to-earth. Some want to leave a legacy, others to travel, still others to live in Japan. If they know what they want, they want shrimp, but our present society only offers them paella.

As we grow older we keep dreaming in the same way, seeing the paths ahead of us. Unless you are lucky and learn to dream, or want to go further, most of the people I meet are only capable of seeing what can be seen from their own starting-point.

For example, when a young man wants to know what professional career to choose, first he reads a list of existing university courses, then chooses one from it. He might choose law, because he likes to fight for just causes. But he does it from a list instead of searching inside his heart. This young man has not asked himself what ingredients he wants in his life. Perhaps if we asked him, we would find that in addition to that, he wants to travel, hates suits and bureaucracy and loves the countryside. From this starting-point there are multiple professional careers he might choose which are just as worthy as being a lawyer, and which will probably provide him with a life more in tune with his ingredients: his values, his needs and his wishes. Not knowing how to dream is what produces all those professionals who tell us they made the wrong choice.

Another example: I always wanted to be rich. Nowadays it is not so much that I do not want to be - of course I still do - but I do not need it any longer because one day I asked myself what I would do if I were rich, and I discovered that what I would do would be very much like the life I already have. I would go on working, I love what I do, I would write books, I would have no schedule, I would play sports in the morning, go to the park with my children in the afternoon, apart from other things like giving a lot of presents to the people I love or traveling a lot. Nearly all the things I would do if I had a lot of money I am already doing. My dream of being rich had certain ingredients. If I just pick the ingredients and forget the idea, I already have everything I want.

THE HERO'S
journey

**"The cave you fear to enter holds the treasures
you seek."**

Joseph Campbell

All of us, deep down, know where our way is. Or rather, we know where
it is NOT.

What happens is that sometimes we bury it underneath reason. Or we
are not alert to the signs life offers us again and again. If we do not pay
attention, then we choose the least appropriate ways.

Joseph Campbell was an American teacher and writer known for his
studies in Mythology. Fascinated by history, he found a common pattern
in stories from all over the world which he called *The Hero's Journey*, and
which he published in his well-known book *The Hero with a Thousand
Faces*. This work became even more famous when the movie director
George Lucas admitted he had closely followed the developmental stages
of the hero in his script for *Star Wars*, in which he touches very deep,
ancestral wellsprings of the human soul.

In our life we all have to go through different stages which are something
like tests we have to pass and challenges which keep us growing. This
process of growth happens in real life, although sometimes we do not
even realize it, and the world of fiction has often made use of this, as in the

cinema, or in the so-called *Bildungsroman* or novel of learning, a literary genre which was particularly cultivated in Germany during the Romantic period and which shows the development of a character during the transition from childhood to adulthood.

Campbell divides the hero's journey into twelve stages in which different tests appear, one after the other. It begins with the hero in his everyday life, out of which (for whatever reason) the flame of adventure suddenly erupts. The character normally goes through moments of doubt about what awaits him. Meanwhile he gains allies, passes tests of courage, gains rewards and grows as a person. It is also very important (and this goes for our own lives as well) to know that at some point he will go through crises which may even imperil his life, and it is not unusual for the hero literally to have to go down into hell in order to accomplish his mission or rescue his beloved. Nevertheless, this difficult moment before death is resolved at last with a resurrection from which he emerges strengthened and reaches the point he was supposed to. The final step is when the hero goes back to his home with the elixir, treasure, love, wisdom or whatever it may be that inspired him to make his journey.

The hero's journey has a lot to do with the search for a life true to oneself, because if we look for a better life we will always have to leave our home and our routine in order to achieve it. And we will also have to be ready to pay the price.

The call of adventure is that itch we feel at some moment when we know perfectly well that this is not the life we dreamed of, or the one we deserve. And when we think about leaving our routine we feel rejection towards what deep down we know we have to do. Many people remain in those three stages forever, in their normal life, which is not really theirs at all, simply the one they are living instead of living the one which is their very own, feeling the call over and over again and rejecting it so as to start all over again in the everyday world.

And why are there some who reject it? Because they know they will have to pay a high price, the price of taking the first step, and that on the way they will find tests, allies and enemies, that there will be battles to be fought, and that the last one will probably be the most difficult because you will be exhausted when you arrive. But if the hero does not give up, if the hero endures, in the end he will attain his treasure.

Not long ago I met another mother in the park. Her children and mine began to play together, and we started to talk. I told her about my coaching, how I had left computer science a few years before, and that although the going had been tough, I now felt very happy. She was thirty-five, she said she had made a mistake in her profession, that what she was doing was not what she wanted but that now it was too late. At thirty-five she had concluded it was too late to start again and preferred to remain in her ordinary life forever. My heart bled for her. Bearing in mind that our current lifespan is over eighty and that in the near future it may not be as easy to retire as it is now, she has at least another thirty-five years of working life left: the only thirty-five years she has left, and she will have lived most of her life doing something she does not like. And at the hour of her death she will go on lamenting something she was already lamenting at thirty-five: not living the life she truly wants.

In search of opportunities

Many years ago while I was in Cuba sharing food, drink and laughter with my friends, one of them arrived with the news that a certain José had finally been able to reunite his whole family in Miami.

Everyone there was overjoyed. They started hugging each other and drinking the health of José and his family, and then they told me his story.

José was a lifelong friend of theirs from their village, and they had shared many things with him. But José, like many others, felt that in Cuba he had too hard a life, and he did not want to go on like that. He wanted more out of life, a better future for his family.

In those days, around the beginning of the millennium, working opportunities were scarce in Cuba, and to leave the island legally you needed a work contract abroad or a marriage. There was also the option of a raft to cross the 90 miles that separate Cuba from Miami. At that time, and even now in 2016, the law of Cuban adjustment was applicable in the US, by which if a Cuban citizen manages to reach US soil he has the right to a series of aid measures to help him settle while he finds a job.

But at that time telling anybody that you were intending to leave Cuba could be very dangerous. A lot of people were informants for the Cuban government, and you never knew who you could or could not trust.

José felt he had to leave, but to get on a precarious Cuban-built raft would be very dangerous, and to pay for a decent motorboat would take a lot of money. He did neither. He managed to get hold of enough money to pay for a boat to take him close to the coast of Florida, but he would have to make the rest of the journey by swimming. Nor did he have enough money for his family, only for himself.

He told his family in Fomento that he was going to Trinidad to fish and to sell his catch as he had done many times before so as to make some money to bring home, but his real intention was very different. That night he boarded a boat that took him close to Miami. He had to do the rest of the journey snorkeling.

When he reached the coast he took off his neoprene suit, flippers and goggles, and with them in his hands he walked barefoot until he found a police station, where he could start to get his papers in order. Unaware of what was going on, his wife and his daughter were sleeping at home, with no idea how long it would be before they saw their husband and father again. Once his papers were sorted out José called his nephew, who was already in Miami, to come and pick him up, and from his house he called a friend, because there was no phone in his family's house in Fomento.

—"Patxi, hi! It's José. Can you go to my house and tell my wife I'm in Miami? Tell her to give me a while, then I'll go back for her."

—"Sure, José. You're in Miami."

—"That's right, I'm in Miami."

After they had argued back and forth for a while, Patxi ended up believing it and went to tell his wife. It would be three years before José could put together enough money. He worked from sunrise to sunset, Mondays to Sundays, tiling bathrooms non-stop. Three years without telling his daughter a bedtime story, without holding her in his arms, without seeing her face or hearing her laughter. Three years without his wife's embrace in the small hours. Three years until the day he put together the money they were demanding of him so that another boat could go for his family. A safe boat, the kind that cost a lot of money, the kind that gets as far as the coast so that nobody needs to get their feet wet. A first-class boat.

The day José was reunited with his family, three years later, I was in Cuba. And although I had never heard of him, although I knew nothing of his struggle, or his courage, I too shared the excitement of knowing they were together. And I cried for joy at the thought of the three embracing each other, and the fact that after three years José's daughter would be able to go to sleep in her father's arms that night.

I have never seen José, but I have him as a friend on Facebook. He now lives in New York and has a life with all modern comforts. I see photos of him and his family, and every time he appears, even if only for a moment, I feel a little braver. José made his own hero's journey in order to have his whole family together, in a land which offered him the opportunities he knew he deserved. But to make that journey he had to pay the price of spending three years away from what he loved most.

A little further beyond

"The darkest moments are always those before dawn. There comes a moment in life in which we have to play on the edges and take great risks. There comes a moment in which every seeker knows, deep down in his heart, that refusing to take the risk means becoming resigned to a life of mediocrity. But to take the leap, even though it couples great fear with great courage, will allow you to travel to a totally new world. A world of potential, happiness, and freedom. Go deep and listen to your inner voice. Then trust its advice. Life wanes or waxes according to the courage of the person."

Anaïs Nin.

Joseph Campbell's hero's journey practically reaches its end with the last battle. For some reason, in life as in stories, the last battle is always the hardest.

When we believe there is no solution, when despair dwells in us, if we are very attentive, if we look around us, we will be able to see that some light always appears, a force which will allow us to go a little further beyond, and it may well be that the solution we are looking for, or perhaps even our treasure, will be there. The one that is at the back of the cave you fear so much.

These vacation mornings in Fomento I get up very early, earlier than the others in the house, and for about an hour I go for a walk and a run. The first day I chose one of the paths they had suggested to me and I ended up at a dump site. I had taken a wrong turn, but you could not see the dump site from afar.

When I asked, they recommended another path to me. I tried it the next day. On that path, on the way out of the village, are some isolated little houses, and as everywhere around, children and animals run free, with no first-world restrictions. No ropes or cages for the animals and no walls for the children, which gives more freedom to the adults as well, as they do not have to spend time searching out places for things that know how to find the right place in the world all by themselves, just as they have been doing since the beginning of time.

I start walking and running at whatever pace my body lets me. It has been a long time since I have taken any exercise. Every once in a while a man on horseback, or on a bicycle, passes me by. The singing of birds accompanies me and the vultures fly above, taking advantage of the thermal currents to avoid having to flap their wings. The mountains, the so-called Juana's

Tits, keep watch over my way. The peace is infinite, I have already been in digital silence for a few days, and as the days go by that silence allows me to listen to my own voice more clearly, something I have forgotten to do for so long.

I must have been en route for about half an hour, I can almost start turning back, when suddenly, in front of my feet, a bog blocks the way. The wheels of a truck or a tractor must have got stuck, it is almost impossible to go on without getting mud up to my ankles. I decide to turn back, but then I sense that my inner voice is speaking to me. All it says is one thing: *The best things are often to be found past the hardest step.* I decide to go on in spite of the mud. I cross the bog as best I can and keep running. After the next curve a wonderful view appears before my eyes: a beautiful stream between little valleys, with a little bridge over the water. My voice, the voice of my being, of intuition, was right, the best thing lay beyond the hardest step.

It was so beautiful that I sat down for a while to listen to the sound of the water, to feel the breeze, to feel my own breathing and the sensation of tiredness in my body. I thought this is what life is like, like my morning walks.

Sometimes the path we thought was most beautiful, most appropriate, takes us to a dump. But we will not know, nor be able to make a better choice, unless we try that route. Sometimes the most important victories, the most beautiful things, the greatest thrills, are beyond the hardest step. That step you have to take when you are already tired, when you think you have gone far enough, that you need to turn back, that there is no need to go on. Sometimes with one small effort more we find the greatest rewards. And the best you can do meanwhile is to enjoy the way, and learn everything it shows you.

Living without fear

I have always found my greatest treasures in the cave I was afraid to go into. In my life this applies perfectly, because I have always had to go a little further beyond fear. But before doing it I have had to think about it for a long, long, long time. The more afraid I was, the more time I had to think about it. Before the entrance to some caves, before the barrier of fear, I have been paralyzed for years before I ever dared to go in.

When at last I have been able to come out of that paralysis and cross the threshold of the cave, the curtain of fear, I have always been surprised by what has happened. Behind that fear there has always been a world much more like the one I dreamed about. For a while perhaps my ground trembled a little under my feet, I did not feel it was firm, but the light was brighter, my lungs had more capacity and my heart beat more strongly.

We have two kinds of fear: those which genuinely protect us from crossing a highway at rush hour, for example, and then the others, which stop us from leaving our comfort zone, from losing what we have, from going a little further beyond, from doing the things we do not usually do, from being too visible.

Hundreds of fears which keep us behind the barrier. Hundreds of fears which stop us reaching the place our soul is crying out for. Because the soul is what decides what it wants to do, but if fear prevents it then you have nothing, since life is made up of your actions.

We think that by staying still and doing nothing we are not taking risks, we are not paying the price of the journey, that doing nothing comes free of charge. But it is a lie, we are paying a price too for doing nothing, and that price is frustration. The frustration of the mother in the park, who gets up every day thinking she went wrong, that it is already too late, and that probably she will get up thinking that same thing for the 12,775 days she has left of her working life. Many, like her, think they are safe like this, but not moving is like being in a boat adrift. It does not appear to move, but the tides make it rock and shift. And how does a sailor adrift feel?

Living always comes at a price, no matter what we may do. Whether or not we move, whether we overcome our fears or live with them. When we face up to them we pay the price of working hard, of stumbling, of having to get up again with bruised knees, of making mistakes, of having to correct our course. If we do not face up to them we pay the price of frustration, and the knowledge that our true life is slipping away from us while we are living a life that is not our own.

And when fear is prowling around, we tend to slam on the brakes and put a blindfold over our eyes. Then we start to think it is already too late, that we can no longer change, and we let the 12,775 days of our past decide the 12,775 days of our future. Like the young woman in the park, who goes on her way without realizing that it does not matter what she may have lived. That she alone is the one who can decide her future, and that at any moment she will be able to redefine it at her own convenience.

The sin of letting
the kiss of her life escape

"If I could go back, if I only had one day, one day alone, I'd go back to the moment when Paco, my first boyfriend, took my hand. I was 13 and he was 14, and he'd come to my village to spend time with a relative of his. He was dark-haired, very handsome, and he had stunning olive-green eyes.

"We spent weeks, months maybe, looking at each other during the dances and events the local priest used to organize. And sometimes I'd catch him looking at me from some hidden corner.

"Dancing close to each other was beginning to come into fashion in my village, though it was frowned upon and kissing was considered a sin. Later on they stopped worrying about that particular sin, but I lived through a time which was very bad for that.

"We started talking to each other in secret, more and more, I don't know how we managed, but I remember the square was empty and we were talking, sitting on a bench, and he asked me if I wanted to be his girl. I said yes at once, I couldn't imagine a better life than spending it beside those green eyes and the freckles across his nose.

"One day I was riding my bike along a path and came upon him walking. I got off the bike and we walked together, giggling with silly laughter the way people do when they're in love. Suddenly he took my hand. I thought my heart was going to jump out of my mouth, I don't think I've ever been so nervous in my life. If I could live one day of my life all over again, I've no doubt I'd choose that one.

"It was the first time we'd been away from people's eyes, there was nobody on the path, we were very close and I suddenly saw his mouth coming to meet

mine. I felt so much fear of God, of sin, of the way my heart was beating like a drum, that I jumped back, grabbed my bike and pedaled back to the village. I don't think my legs have ever moved so fast.

"It was wartime, round about 1937. That summer I didn't see him again. I only knew he came from Madrid and I didn't know which relative's house he was staying in; I could never ask after him. I waited for years, there wasn't any young man I liked, I always compared them with my Paco. In the end I started going out with a young man from the village, and he ended up being my husband. I saw Paco many years later, at the village fair, me with my husband and he with what I assume was his wife. We said hello very civilly, even though my heart was jumping around inside me like that day on the bike. There was a lot of love in his eyes too, very sweet and loving. I saw him four times more, once every four or five years, and then I never heard of him again.

"He's been the love of my life, I never ever felt anything like it. I know things would've been the same, that probably the war would've separated us, but if I could go back to that day I wouldn't be nervous and I wouldn't run away on my bike.

"Even if it was a sin, if I could choose now, I'd burn in hell for that kiss. I've already done penance for it all my life because of running away."

Amelia, 92 years old.

I HAVE
vs I decide

"The greatest discovery of any generation is that a human being can change his life by changing his attitude."

William James

I believe that our best gift is not life in itself, but the freedom to do whatever we want with it. Ever since I was little I have heard on many occasions that life is hard, that we must struggle, that it is a vale of tears, that nothing is easy. But over the years, with my experience, with all I have learned from my studies in personal development (coaching, NLP, emotional intelligence, psychology), with all my clients' experiences of life, I know that life is more or less hard according to what we choose.

I have also often heard people saying "that's my luck", as if when we were born we took part in a raffle of "lives" where everything is already written. But even in the worst circumstances we encounter cases of people who, in spite of what their "luck" may be, they feel that they have the capacity to choose, and that they are not on the fringe of things.

There are examples of truly terrible situations, like Viktor Frankl's experience in a concentration camp, where it is clear that freedom is an inner state and that we can always choose between freedom and slavery. Mr. Frankl was held prisoner in several concentration camps during WWII, and he came to the conclusion that everything can be taken away from a man, except for one thing: the choice of a personal attitude, when confronted by a combination of circumstances, so as to create one's own path. *Man's Search for Meaning*, in my view, ought to be recommended reading in all schools.

Another example I love is Roberto Benigni's film *Life is beautiful*, where Guido and his son Giosué are taken to a concentration camp during WWII. During their entire captivity Guido makes his son believe that instead of being prisoners they are there in a competition, and that if they do very well in it they will win a tank. Even in the worst situations Guido transforms his son's reality, turning what might have been a traumatic experience into a game for the boy. Guido chose freedom, assumed responsibility and created his own reality. He also gave his son a magical childhood under the worst possible circumstances.

When we take on that freedom we also assume the responsibility not only of choosing our actions but also of choosing our thoughts and our attitude. And although at times this is a painful path because now you have "won" nothing, now you are the one who chooses, in the face of everything that happens to you, the attitude you wish to show.

WHEN WE DO NOT KNOW
what the way is

**"Caterpillars call the birth
of a butterfly a crisis"**

(Anónimo)

This book is dedicated to my dear friend Yram Marrero, one of my favorite people in the whole world. When I first met Yram more than a decade ago he was a family photographer in Cuba, but it was a job he did not like. In Cuba, when girls turn fifteen the event is celebrated in a very special way. They call it *la quinceañera*, and among other things it involves a photo-shoot in which the girls wear amazing clothes and take photos of each other that look like something out of a fashion magazine - or even, sometimes, an erotic one.

Yram was tired of this job. It did not satisfy him, he found no meaning in it, he found it repetitive, he got bored. He did not know what he was looking for, he only knew that the photos of *la quinceañera* was not what he wanted. Yram earned money, he had a comfortable life, he had no shortage of clients, he did a good job and his life was very secure. But in spite of everything, he knew it was not to his taste and he could not spend the rest of his life doing the same thing.

As he is a very wise man, he does not need sudden scares to know that life is limited. He decided long ago that he had to find his own way. Even though he was conscious of the difficulties this entailed, since his two children were dependent on him and his wife Yenellys.

He decided to stop taking family photos in order to try other things. It was not an easy decision for either him or Yenellys, because both of them knew that the economic pressures would disappear the moment he went back to taking family photos. Yram nearly gave up many times in the face of pressure both from his family and from society. But every time he talked about it with Yenellys she told him not to do it, that they would survive, that she supported him, that he should follow his own path, that she trusted him, that she knew he would find it.

Meanwhile Yenellys was working in an art gallery, and Yram was looking for other opportunities as he went in search of the inspiration he needed. Time went by as he tried different temporary jobs and also went out fishing. In Trinidad, where they live, there are plenty of fish, and Yram would often come home with a nourishing catch. Their story is that they ate a great deal of fish for several years while this situation lasted. For lunch and for dinner, practically every day of the week and practically every week and every month. Some days, they say, they even thought they would start to grow scales themselves. But something told them it was still better than denying themselves.

The years went by and Yram went on creating new opportunities for himself and finding jobs he liked, the meaning of his life. At the moment he produces documentaries in Cuba. Among them is *The Timeless City,* a documentary about Trinidad that I love because it manages to touch everyone through the story it tells.

True, he does not have the best material at hand to make them, but he manages with what he has, even though he works far more than he needs to. He does it under the name of *Short Producciones.* The logo was designed by Yenellys. The name comes from the fact that Yram always wears shorts, and on one occasion he was not allowed into the Curator's

Office (which among other things is in charge of proposing and carrying out restoration plans and looking after the conservation of the historic heritage of the city). It is all very much their own, with all the love they always put into whatever they do and whatever they create.

Now he makes good money, and most importantly, he can now have a more varied diet.

When I look at him I feel proud of him, of being his friend; I feel proud that he loves me just as I love him. When I look at Yenellys I feel the same, proud to know her, proud that she is my friend, that she is my friend's wife as well as my husband's friend. I feel proud that Fate has given them to me as a gift, that I have been able to enjoy people as brave as this, who do not mind losing unimportant things and eating a lot of fish so as to earn the essential life for themselves, the true one. Because making money doing what you really want is to gain life, whereas making money doing what you do not want, doing what does not come from your heart - even though it might mean a stable life - is to lose it.

Tonight Yram and Yenellys have invited us to dinner. There will be lobster on the table. Lobster has no scales, it has a strong, hard shell.

Moral: if you do not want to eat beans all your life you have to go fishing, even though the moment may come when you think you are going to grow scales yourself. If you hold fast long enough to reach the light, then lobster will follow.

THE COMFORT ZONE
vs the steps of life

"Tell him yes.
Even if you are dying of fear,
even if you are sorry later,
because whatever you do you will be sorry
all the rest of your life if you say no."

Gabriel García Márquez
(Love in the Time of Cholera)

Many people I come across in the course of life link coaching with leaving your comfort zone and joke about it. In fact one of the commonest jokes is: "Why would I leave my comfort zone if I feel perfectly fine in it? I'm not moving from here."

As a good coach I return the question, or smile and say nothing. I cannot be constantly justifying my beliefs, and everyone has a right to live their own life as they please. It has been a hard thing for me to learn, but as time goes by it is the position I feel most comfortable with.

Although in fact it is a necessity for me to leave my comfort zone constantly, to better myself and reach new goals, above all to manage to see more things all the time. The metaphor I like best is that of the ladder.

And in fact every time we overcome new challenges in our life, achieve new goals, it is as if we had climbed up a step on an imaginary ladder. And every time we go up another step, because we are higher we see further, and when we climb the next we see even more. And when you see further you also have more choices. We might make a similar metaphor with maps, so that we would have the map of my village on the first step, so that I can see the different streets and directions I can choose.

The second step would reveal the map of the region, which would show me that there are other villages I could visit. We do not need to go, we can choose, but we know they are there. The next step, in my case, might be the map of the island of Mallorca, the fourth perhaps the map of Spain, the sixth the map of Europe and from there to infinity and beyond. Not much more than a hundred years ago very few people, if anyone, imagined we would be able to fly, or to walk on the moon. Now we believe we are capable of that and of much more, because as a society, with everyone's contribution, we have gone on climbing steps, and our maps and our options are bigger all the time.

If we go up a step, then we feel we can go up another, and another, and another. If we do not leave our comfort zone, if we always stay on the same step, we will always see the same view. It might be that if we go up another step what we see a little further up might not be to our taste, or might not be what we wanted. But once you have gone up you cannot come down again to where you were before because you know more things, you see more things, so that you can either stay with what you do not like or go on upward.

When should we leave our comfort zone? When should we go up another step? I do not have the answer to this; only you have it. If you are at a moment in your life where you feel comfortable, where you like what you see from the step you are standing on, you feel no discomfort in your body because of it, you feel you already have what you were looking for, that you are achieving your goal... well then, I suppose in your case there is no reason for you to go further, broaden your maps, search for new goals.

If on the other hand you feel this is not the life you were expecting, you feel discomforts like knots in your stomach or lumps in your throat, you cannot get up in the morning because your life makes you feel lazy, or anything of the kind... you do not like what you see from your step, then that is not the one you should stay on. Perhaps if you went a little further up you might see new places and consider other options which would allow you to live a life well lived. Let me remind you once again that one of these days you are going to die.

Then, in the ranking of my world, there are other people (myself among them) who when they are standing on one particular step, even though they may like what they see, are constantly asking themselves: what will we be able to see from the next step? And climbing steps is the place where they find their own happiness. Or at least, that is how it has been in my own life up till now.

There was another life I once had

I trained in coaching in 2008. At that time I had a good job as an IT consultant, a generous salary and prestige. In society's terms, I had succeeded. Many people congratulated me. But I could not help feeling that these congratulations had nothing to do with me. This was not my success, it was not what my being truly wanted, it was not what I felt I had to do in the world, I did not feel the call. I always had to carry a cell phone with me, and sometimes outside my working hours I would be called by a client I could not understand. The man concerned was a great guy, but for some reason if

I did not have him in front of me I could not understand what he said. Just the sight of his name on the screen made me break into a sweat.

People could call me at any time; they scarcely ever did, but they could, so that I always had to carry my phone with me. Because in my area of expertise there were computer systems in operation, we had machines and processes programmed to send constant information about their status. Messages reached my phone all the time, with the machines letting me know whether they were well, whether they had finished their work, whether they were at 80% capacity, and even whether they were stressed. Did you know that databases get stressed? Yes, they do, and in my previous job when this happened they sent me a text message.

I used to love Fridays because that meant I was done with work, if I was lucky, for the whole weekend. I worked for somebody else for sixteen years of my life. During that time I always found myself missing my home. The hours at home were not enough to let me enjoy myself. On Sunday afternoon I felt very sad, as I saw my parole coming to an end. Monday mornings were agony, and then by Tuesday I was already used to the routine again.

When I went to meetings dealing with issues which had far-reaching implications for the company, I always felt it was like playing Monopoly. Buying and selling fake houses under rules that were not mine, but those set by the owner of Monopoly. I did not play with my money, I did not play with the truth, I got paid the same whether I did well or not. But in the meetings I managed fake money, budgets which involved thousands of fake Euros, fake projects that were carried out and subsequently worked or failed to work. I was just a single nut in an incomprehensible structure which grew bigger all the time, more complicated all the time: that was how I felt working for a big company. People were referred to as resources, programmers, analysts... I knew the rules well and played by them, but there was something in me that was disconnected from reality, from my self, just like when you play Monopoly. I, who had always known that inside me there lived a woman of many colors, felt like a gray professional.

I thought that was normal life. That it was life, the life you had to want. Yes, I had a good salary, I was well-regarded, I had a secure job. That was what I thought I had to do to earn my living, but I felt I was losing it. I had what people are supposed to have, a red carpet. But by midday on Sunday I was already beginning to be sad because the next day I had to go to work. Monday mornings I felt that this perfect life was crushing my innards, and I had to force myself to breathe deeply to see whether I could manage to get some oxygen into my constricted soul.

I do not manage it every week, but I often do. There are even times when I get to spend nearly a whole week at home. This makes me immensely happy.

As time goes by I have learnt that for me, money is not the most important thing in my life, and that one thing does not clash with the other. That working at home, doing what I like, does not clash with earning a good salary, and that a secure life, if it is unhappy, has no meaning, however safe it may be.

We all work to make money so that we can live, but we do not always ask ourselves what the cost is.

The good thing about making dreams come true, at least in my case, is that each time we uncover bigger dreams, and then we can never stop again. Now I have new dreams because I have climbed new steps, and what I see is no longer the same. I used to dream about leaving my job, and when I turned to coaching I went up that step. Now I dream about devoting more time to writing, to creating environments where others too can achieve their dreams. But I can only see all this because I have climbed more steps, new steps. If I had stayed down there I would never have seen them, because my vision of the world was Monopoly and dreaming about leaving that job, which I would probably have stayed in until I retired.

A FULL LIFE
is the best medicine

**"*If you don't find it inside yourself,*
where are you going to find it?"**

Alan Watts

Having a full life protects you from many of the pains of the world. During the last few years my work, my life, my trips, my way of being, have made me cross paths with and learn many things about hundreds of people. Most of those who are unhappy around me are so for lack of a full life, of a life they have chosen, a mission to be accomplished, a vision to pursue. Because living according to our values, living with love, is what causes the stones we find on our path to be simply that, just stones, and not black holes that paralyze our growth in life.

From empty nest syndrome to fighting over inheritances, depression, insomnia, endless grieving for the deaths of close relatives, the end of some romantic relationship, everlasting fights with family, friends, or neighbors: if you are permanently worried about any of these things, if you have a pain you cannot manage to overcome, it is probably because you do not have the life you were really born for, the one that in the depths of your heart you either wish for or used to wish for.

If you are more concerned about everything going on around you, about what your neighbors or your friends are doing, if you suffer as a result of envy, or gossip, if you are at daggers drawn with your friends, or with the majority of your relatives, it may be the moment to look inside yourself, the moment when you know that you are going to die, that your time is limited and that it might come to an end at any moment. Perhaps if you are able to live it, even for just a single moment, able to know you are mortal, you might wake up and start living that second life which for many people begins when they have been on the brink of dying. You do not need to reach that point: you, all by yourself, can change your way of thinking.

If you have been able to build a meaningful life for yourself, you will succeed in overcoming any grief that comes your way. You will cry for a while, you will suffer, but one day you will decide that you have already cried enough and you will look up again. If you already have the life you wish, you will come to the conclusion that it is not worth arguing with people you love, that it is not worth sharing your time with people who hurt you, and you will ignore those who have nothing better to do than pester you. If you already have it, material things will have the importance which is due to them and you will not cling on to anything that might make you suffer. You will choose the freedom of detachment, rather than the suffering of attachment to what you do not have.

The good news is that there is always time left for you to lead a full life. The bad news is that you are the only person capable of taking that step, and if you do not do it yourself, nobody else will do it for you. You have to do it by yourself.

CATCH YOUR TRAIN,
young rumí

*"The hodja came looking for me. 'Listen, young
rumí,' he says, 'come with me.' 'No, I won't go,'
I replied. 'Where are you trying to take me?'
'The daughter of a Baha, fresh as spring water,
awaits you in her bower, young rumí, come!' But
knowing they cut the throats of Christians who
dared roam the Turkish neighborhoods at night,
I told him: 'No, I'm not coming!' 'What! Doesn't
the fear of God breathe in your chest, giaour?'
'Why would I fear?' 'Because, young rumí, that
man who wants to lie with a woman and does
not, commits a great sin. If a woman invites you
to share her bed, and you refuse to satisfy her
desire, you lose your soul! That woman will heave
a sigh on God's great judgment day, and that
woman's sigh, whoever you may be and however
much your worthy actions may weigh in your
favor, yes, I tell you, the breath of that sigh will
be enough to throw you headfirst into hell!'*

Zorba sighed.

*"If hell exists," he said, "I will not be free
from falling into it and the only cause of my
damnation will have been that. Not because of*

*having robbed, murdered, committed adultery,
no, no! None of that means anything. God
forgives it. But I must throw myself into hell only
because that night a woman waited for me and I
never came..."*

*He got up, lit the fire, made lunch. He looked at
me out of the corner of his eye and smiled dis-
dainfully.*

*"There's none so deaf as those who will not hear,"
he said.*

*And bending over, he began to blow furiously on
the damp timber.*

Nikos Kazantsakis (Zorba, El Griego)

Do not think you have missed all the trains. Do not think there are no more opportunities left for you, do not think everything is lost; as long as there is a breath of life left in you, there is still time to live the life you want, the one you have always run away from. Yes, I mean you, this brief chapter is for you. The one who is looking the other way at this moment, thinking that you cannot. Yes, it is for you, do not look the other way, I have seen you running away from these words. I know it all. And because I know it all, you are reading this book.

Nothing stops you getting up this very moment and taking your own way, the one you believe you do not deserve, the one you have spent your whole life running away from.

Yes, young woman in the park, you, the one who is living unhappily in that marriage, trapped, experiencing in company the most intense solitude ever imagined. You who feel ill-treated by life, living the fruit of what you consider your mistakes, regretting not having made the right decision at that moment, allowing more and more trains to pass you by. You who are consumed by the frustration of believing yourself to be incapable of dreaming.

You who live in the blindness of only seeing what is around you, paralyzed by your circumstances, immersed in your frustration.

It does not matter what you have. If you concentrate on what you are about to lose, your gaze will turn in that direction and you will be forever anchored to this life you do not want. If you turn your gaze towards what you think you are going to lose, you will not be able to look at everything you will gain if you follow what your heart is shouting at you to do. Close your eyes, and now look at all you will gain if you catch that train.

Because I may not know whether reincarnation exists or not, but I can assure you that hell does. Only that it does not exist after death, as you may believe, it exists in life itself, and that is what you are living right now, at this precise moment. The hell of living somebody else's life. That life that is not your own. And you know it.

So you will have to let me insist once more: yes, you do deserve the life you are running away from. No, you will not mind having lost everything you are going to lose, because what you are going to have will be so great, your satisfaction will be so immense, that in the end you will allow your lungs to fill with oxygen. Once and for all.

And if you need me, here I am, in these words, to remind you once again. Over and over. However often you need me to. So that when you feel faint you can come back here and turn your gaze once again on what you are going to gain in that new life.

chapter four

ABOUT YOUR LIFE BEING YOUR WORK

*"I must find a truth
that is true for me."*

Søren Kierkegaard

Silvia was an interior designer. She worked very well, and almost from nowhere her small business grew and grew.

She enjoyed a prosperous company in Madrid, she was showered with commissions and never stopped working. As time went on she had more and more projects, and her vision of the world, her goal, the place her sight was fixed on, were those that enabled her to create the perfect space, with the perfect contents, for the people who had hired her.

The days flew by, and with them went all of her time. She got up very early, almost at dawn, and by the time she realized it the day was over and she had done fewer than half the things on her to-do list. The things she had to do, the things she had to control so that everything would be perfect: she was like a titan.

She had vowed to have a job finished by that particular day; only details remained to be fixed. The work included the bathrooms. When the workers were ready to fix the toilets they realized the screws were no good for screwing the toilets to the wall. Silvia looked everywhere, she called all her contacts, but getting the screws she wanted for that day was practically impossible. All of a sudden, she says, she started to feel her heart beating irregularly and to feel that that the air was not filling her lungs properly, that there was not enough of it to breathe. That day she ended up in Emergencies with an anxiety attack. When she realized, when she was able to see it all from a proper distance, she suddenly became aware that she was in a robe in a hospital bed because of an anxiety attack brought on by a toilet screw.

For her, she says, this was as though life had given her a slap, and it was a wake-up call for her. Silvia de la Colina now lives in Ibiza, part of the year on a boat. At present she works in coaching and has the odd interior design project, always providing there are no toilet screws involved.

YOUR PROBLEM
is not time management

*"The moment doesn't exist,
only the past or the future.
Because now, for example, this moment...
when I speak of it,
it's already past."*

Michael Ende (Momo)

Rivers of ink have flowed on the subject of time management, to feed the reading hours of thousands and millions of people around the world. Different systems to manage it with, with their corresponding books, experts and apps. As on so many occasions, we search for the answer outside. "If I don't have time to do all the things I have to do, I must be doing something wrong. I'll have to learn to manage myself better. With this time management tool I'm sure to have time at the end of the day to go for a run, or relax."

This may have been a solution for some people, but in most cases the problem comes from inside and cannot be fixed with any app or course. It might make for slight improvements, but the basic problem will still be there. For some it lies in thinking that the day is infinite and piling on more things than they can do in a day. For others the problem is that work is their priority, perhaps because they do not take a proper look at their personal life, or perhaps because they love it, or for any other of the infinite number of reasons I could go on to list.

Each day has twenty-four hours, and weeks are seven days long. That is where all the tasks you have to do in your work have to fit. But apart from that, you also have to fit in all the other things that are important to you: your family, your diet, your fitness, friends, time by yourself, personal care, sleep.

The problem with most of the people I work with (and I include myself in that group) is not time management. Let us imagine that we put all the things we have to do in a bag. According to the life we live nowadays, we put in so many things that the bag ends up weighing too much and we cannot lift it. When we face time management it is as if we started turning that four-hundred-pound bag we have filled round and round because we are now unable to lift it and carry it on our back.

The problem is usually not the management of time but the management of tasks, which is just a sign on the surface that deep down, what is really lacking is the management of our life. And working on that same aspect of my own life is what I am currently engaged on.

"I REGRET
having worked so hard."

— "How far we are!" he sighed.
— "Far from what?"
— From ourselves.

**Gabriel García Márquez
(Of Love and Other Demons)**

According to Bronnie Ware, one of the things people usually regret when they are dying is having worked too hard.

Here I can feel my future self looking at me with a mixture of understanding, accusation and warning. In my house, in my family, work has always been the most important thing. When I was little, if I said I had a test my mother immediately let me off any domestic task that might get in the way of my studying. This was a double-edged weapon, because she knew that if she gave me things to do I would say I had to study, and then she would send me directly to pore over my books. Very smart people, mothers.

This has been a constant in my life, from adolescence to the present day. If there is work to do, work comes before anything else in the world. It comes before feeding myself properly, before playing sports, before being with my family, with my children, my other half, with my friends. For years work has come first: always, in every case. Until this year.

This is the challenge I am working on now, for the first time in my life. Because although for years studies have shown that happiness lies in balance, we do not see it until it is our turn. Until the pupil is ready, the master does not appear. Not because the master is not there but because the pupil does not see him, and probably until now it has not been the moment for me.

I do not know what your secret is, but for me it consists of changing focus. If previously work was "the priority", now my priority is balance. And assuming that since there are only twenty-four hours in the day and for years I have not deprived sleep of any minutes, work suffers and I can take on fewer things. Fewer clients, fewer moves, fewer meetings, fewer meals. What I try to do is keep the best clients, the best projects, the right meetings and the meals that are necessary. What is curious about this is that when you look at the final result of all these adjustments you realize nothing has happened, you are still earning money, your work is still good and the world has not collapsed in ruins.

Let us go on looking into this subject.

BUT WHEN
should we work hard?

*"Because time is life.
And life dwells in the heart."*

Michael Ende (Momo)

There are moments when one has to give it all one has, when the priority is work, but if we analyze each of the phases of our life we will realize that we cannot make it into a way of living.

One day I'll be a pilot

"One day I'll be a pilot." This is what ten-year-old Juanjo Martín said to himself when he looked up at the sky and saw a plane flying overhead. He had never been on a plane, he had never seen a pilot, he did not know what clothes they wore or what an airplane looked like inside. Nor had there been much opportunity for him to, as he had been born into a very humble family.

From that moment his whole life began to revolve around this crazy idea that had taken root in his mind. He started asking here and there, and found out that if he wanted to be a pilot he had to obtain a license that cost a great deal of money. Ten million of the old pesetas, a fortune for a boy in those circumstances. He left school at the age of sixteen to start work.

He worked as a waiter all summer, and sometimes even juggled two or three jobs at a time. He lived in Palma de Mallorca but worked at El Arenal, which is between six and twelve miles from Palma. He finished work very late at night and by then there were no more buses. He did not want to take a taxi home, because the ride he would have to pay for would separate him a little more from his dream each time, and he wanted to get closer to it. So at night he slept on the beach hammocks, under a blanket of stars. El Arenal is right next to Palma airport, and from time to time the planes would cross the starry sky above Juanjo on his hammock. He would look at them and think: "One day I'll be in one of those." And then the cool of the night, the tiredness, the solitude, would disappear, and only the dream remained.

Eight years went by like this, until one day Juanjo had his ten million pesetas. Enough to go to Barcelona and join the aviation college so as to get his license. The time he spent studying he lived at a guest house, and says he only had two pairs of pants. The other boys at the college came from wealthy families, and on long weekends and holidays they went skiing or to the beach while Juanjo stayed studying. He was the top student of his year. He always says that the others had more resources, but that he had bigger dreams, and that this was his only opportunity. There was no other. He was staking everything on the one card.

With his license in his pocket he went back home and began the rounds in search of a job to get flying hours. He flew cargo planes and from time to time took tests to try to join some commercial airline. Often he got one of the highest marks, but even then, doors shut in his face. There was always someone who had a pull, or else the examiner had received orders to favor so-and-so's son or somebody else's girlfriend. He even had to leave Mallorca for a while and go to work in Scandinavia, where it was freezing cold, so he could get more flying hours. All those doors that shut in his face could not manage to shut the door on his dreams, and he kept insisting, over and over again, as often as he had to, until he made it.

Nowadays Juanjo is a captain in a leading airline. Sometimes, he says, when he sits in his pilot's seat, he suddenly sees his reflection in the windshield and thinks: "Gee, that's me!" He now flies back and forth, carrying people all over the world, flying through the same blanket of stars he slept beneath so often on the beach, dreaming about his future.

Ungrateful

Sandra is 39, and had worked at a bank since she was 20 when they fired her because of the economic crisis which has hung over Spain and part of the rest of the world for the last few years.

Just as she started college, she began to work in a leading international bank for the summer. The branch was in a tourist area, and she spoke perfect German. She started as a teller, but she worked so well that after the summer they asked her to stay. She worked there for the next nineteen years.

Sandra had never known what she wanted to be when she grew up, but she was a good student. She started an Economics course and thought she would see what she could do with it later. When she started at the bank she thought she would combine work and study, but only tried it for the first year. She went on paying her fees for several years more, but never went to class until she decided not to go on wasting her money.

For a few years she went on rising, step by step, at the bank, working in different positions: operations manager, supervisor, management, mediation and even became a branch manager. She started work very early and left very late. Sometimes even after eight in the evening, when she had started her day very early. She ate whatever was to hand, and at weekends she did some easy light exercise. During the week she would have liked to go to a gym, she even tried, but as with college she found herself paying for it and unable to use its services, so that in the end she gave that up too. She did not have children during this period either, because it was never the right moment, either for her or for her work in the company. There was always a project to be finished, a client whose affairs needed to be sorted out, a possible promotion, and so the years went by.

She took on many responsibilities, she worked efficiently and her bosses were very pleased with her. She felt happy and useful, although she admitted that it left her breathless and with no time for herself.

In the middle of the crisis, after a sale and an economic restructuring, Sandra was fired. She had never fought for a dream of her own, she had not finished college and she had invested the last twenty years in dedicating herself to a company. She was ashamed to have to offer her résumé listing her studies as unfinished. She felt the company she had devoted so much of herself to had been ungrateful to her. And now she wanted to have a child, but at her age it was not so easy.

A triathlete

Joan is 25, an IT engineer. He is very good at his job, and was already working before he finished his studies. Since then he has not changed companies. He has a lot of options, whether to set himself up on his own to create projects with other people or to work elsewhere. In fact he never stops getting new opportunities offered to him. But he always turns them down.

He gets paid every month, he has a good flexible schedule, and he is close to home. He has his work under control, he does it at his own rhythm, any incidents are more or less foreseen and he is well-organized. His bosses trust and respect him.

The fact is that Joan's dream is not his work. Joan's dream is to compete in triathlons. He trains very hard most afternoons and practically every weekend, and he has enough to buy whatever equipment he needs.

He has no obligations. His dream is not of buying a house, or having a luxury car. His whole energy is devoted to the world of triathlons. The job he has allows him to live without worries while he devotes himself to his dream. At work he lives within his comfort zone, within what he has made for himself through his studies and his own decisions. But in his role as an athlete he is perpetually fighting to leave his comfort zone: to run further in a shorter time, or to gain more stamina.

Look at where you invest your life

If I tell you to be careful about what you invest your time in, you will probably give it a little consideration, but you would not regard the question as important. When all is said and done, we go through this world believing our time is infinite.

But if I tell you to really think about what you invest your life in, you will probably give the question a bit more thought, because we do not believe that life is made up of time.

Juanjo worked his guts out for ten years in all kinds of jobs with one clear direction and goal. To be a pilot. And he made it. When we read his story we think he might have had to work hard but that he made the best decision, that it was worth the effort, that he did what he had to do and a lot more than that, because many people would simply have thought the dream was not within reach and given up. If you were watching the movie of Juanjo's life, the moments when he was striving, what would you shout at him from the audience? What would you whisper in his ear when you saw him exhausted, sleeping on the beach after fifteen hours of work? How would you feel, watching this movie? What is your emotion? What color is Juanjo's figure in this movie for you? For my part, imagining it, I would feel hopeful. I would be shouting at him: "You can do it! Go on, you'll make it! You have a dream, don't lose sight of it!"

But what if you were watching Sandra's story? What would you tell her? Most likely each of us would see different things. My mother would tell her not to work so hard and to finish college. Someone else would insist that she should have children, that later on it would be too late, that she should not wait. And I think she should have looked for a dream and invested that time (twenty years of her life is not something to be brushed aside) in her own dream, not in those of other people. But I think that when they read about her story, not many people would encourage Sandra to work her guts out for the bank. Even though her story might end well.

If we were watching Joan through a peephole, if we could advise him from outside, probably the only thing we would do would be to applaud, to get tensed up as we watched him run and hope he came first. If we made a movie about Joan, we would most likely not even mention his job. Everything is fine there, everything is where it ought to be. His work is the perfect mattress which allows him to focus on his dream.

Sandra worked in a bank, but probably she is not a banker. Juanjo works as a pilot, but besides that he IS a pilot. Inside and out. And if he gets fired from his job, he will look for another where he is able to fly. Because that was his dream.

In Juanjo's case, the effort was worthwhile. He must have invested everything in it: hobbies, friends, sleeping hours, sports, time with his family... But it was worth it because that led him to live the life he wanted, it led him to fly, to achieve his dreams, to live a life well lived.

Sandra invested everything, to reap only frustration, dissatisfaction, and a bad after-taste. There was no dream behind it.

Joan is investing all his free time in training. He does it willingly, you see him pass by with a smile on his face. There is no pain for him, his joy is in the effort. Whatever he may invest there, he will probably never regret it because at every moment of his life he has put in the needful effort at the point he judged appropriate, without deviating for a moment from his dream.

There are times when there is nothing you can do but put all your eggs in one basket. These last few years I have worked an enormous amount because I had to start from scratch, and my children still had to eat and the bills kept coming. I had to do it. It has been worth it, now I am beginning to enjoy more time for myself. There was a goal, there was a reason, all this effort has led me to a life better lived.

But how far is it worthwhile to invest more time in order to earn even more money, if you give up other important aspects of your life? How many businessmen and women are there who are in love with money, who have no life, and who do not see beyond that? Or CEOs who see nothing but their company, particularly as for many of them it is not even their own company? Even more, how many CEOs have been fired after many years, left utterly bewildered because they had not realized that the company they worked for was not theirs and that they were building somebody else's dream? Obviously there will be those who are happy, but here we are talking about the others.

The question I want to ask you is: what would you do if you knew you were going to die within the next twenty, thirty or sixty days? Finish that report your boss has ordered? Or that article? Which of the things you are doing in your life would you carry on with if you knew the end was imminent? I might like to finish this book before dying, Juanjo might want to see the Northern Lights from his plane for the last time, we would all want to spend more time with our loved ones, enjoy the outdoors and not to be shut up in an office...

But if your life is filled with things you would not spend one moment more on, then there is something wrong. If you are not doing it to fulfill your dream, whatever that may be, perhaps it is time to reflect. Because I have to warn you that your end is imminent, perhaps more than twenty, thirty or sixty days, or perhaps even less (you never know), but you must know that your own life passes like a sigh.

LOVE
whatever you do

"When you are inspired by an important goal, an extraordinary project, all your thoughts break their bonds: your mind reaches beyond its limitations, your conscience expands in all directions and you see yourself in a new and wonderful world. Strengths, abilities and hidden talents come to life, and you discover you are a better person than you had dreamed of being."

Patanjali, Indian Philosopher.

I can start writing in the small hours, I do not feel lazy. I can go on all morning; if for some reason my family does not come, I even forget to eat. Sometimes they come to see me in the evening and I have not moved from my chair all day. The same thing happens when I edit videos, draw or paint. I forget the world I live in.

I do not mind. I like it. If my life was this, even if it were every day, I would probably die satisfied, even if my working day was ten hours long.

Steve Jobs said in his Stanford speech, which has been an inspiration for millions of people, that he asked himself every day in front of the mirror: "If today was the last day of my life, would I want to do what I'm about to do today? And if for a long time the answer was *no*, he knew he had to change something.

Would I want to write on the last day of my life? The answer is yes. Writing, painting, playing, laughing, being with my children, watching the sunset, or swimming in the sea. These would be my choices, this is a great part of my life now.

Would I want to play Monopoly? Deal with a database's stress? Attend a business meeting? Sign a commercial deal? Not me.

That is why I have decided to do things that I love most days, things I love, things that fill me with passion. And as life is time, and time turns itself into what I do, in the end if I love what I do, I end up having a life I love. A life well lived.

"Dream as if you were going to live forever, live as if you were going to die today."

(attributed to James Dean)

If he were to die today, if today were really the last day of his life, probably Steve Jobs would not have gone to work, Juanjo would not be studying to be a pilot and I would not be writing this book. At this moment one can only focus on love. We can think about becoming a pilot, or writing this book, because we think we will have time to finish it.

If we thought we were going to die any minute, our vision would not be complete and our dreams would be lopsided. Therefore the well-known saying attributed to James Dean, "Dream as if you were going to live forever", adds the essential ingredient to the recipe of the life well lived.

The thing that allows us to think of long-term projects is the belief that we have time ahead of us to complete them. This allows us to create companies, write books, paint pictures, create works of art and erect buildings. We start on these projects not because we are going to die, but because we believe we are going to live. It may even be because we think that even though we may die, the place where we live, the village, the city, the country or the world, will be the legacy we bequeath to our children. That part of what we are doing will influence their lives, and that something will remain of ourselves in our work.

We are now living for longer, and our quality of life is better. Life expectancy in most First World countries is around 80 years. Scientists of the Singularity University, sponsored by Google and NASA, say that in a few decades aging will be reversible and that we will live forever with the body we had at the age of 20. Perhaps some day what I say in this book will join those sayings like "the world is flat", "Finisterre is where the world ends" or "the sun goes around the earth."

This is why I tell you to live intensely, to live a life well lived, that your dreams should be infinite, that the planet you live on should be forever. Whether you die or not, the advice might do you good.

I WISH
I'd allowed myself to be happier.

"*May you live every day of your life.*"

Jonathan Swift

This is another of those "I wishes" that Bronnie Ware wrote about in her book. I wish I had allowed myself to be happier.

But what is happiness? Happiness is an ambiguous term, which has to do with everyone's perception of their world. Some look for it forever, for century after century, and never reach it.

Some believe that happiness is in having. That if they had this bigger house, that more powerful car, or more money for vacations, they would be happier. They say that all of us, whatever we earn, always believe we would be happier making 20% more. Whether we make €800 a month or three million, we all still want to make 20% more.

There are people who search for happiness elsewhere. I remember as a teenager thinking happiness was in my friends; then I thought it was in work, then that it was in a more senior position; when I was a programmer I wanted to get as far as becoming an analyst, when I became an analyst I thought I would become a manager, and so on forever. And I went on taking each of those steps without finding the absolute happiness I was looking for on that path. Arguing with that natural non-conformism, with my curiosity always wondering what the view would be from the next step.

The wrong assumption

Serafín was in his mid-fifties when we started working together. He was very well-known in his field, an outstandingly successful university professor with responsibilities on his shoulders. He had a beautiful wife, Regina, who had loved him deeply for many years, and two sons who had studied at the world's most prestigious universities. One was studying for his doctorate at the time and the other already working with NASA in Hawaii. He lived in a beautiful house with a garden and a pool in one of the best and quietest areas of the city, and close to his workplace into the bargain. The journey took him no more than ten minutes. He was in good shape physically. He seemed to have everything that would make for happiness, and yet when he sat down in front of me he seemed to me the saddest man on earth.

When I asked him what he had come looking for in my coaching, he commented that he wanted to manage his time better. His eyes showed there was something else behind this request. There is always something else.

Two things had led him to call at my door: a slight stroke, and a threat from his wife. Regina had hinted at the possibility of a divorce, and Serafín could not bear the idea of losing her.

He wanted to manage his time better so as to do things with her, to take her out to dinner, for a walk, on excursions. To satisfy once and for all the requests she had always been making and which he had postponed, up till the imminent threat of losing what he most loved.

As far as his sons were concerned, he only knew their professional profiles, and nothing more than that. They never confided anything intimate to him, nothing that was not concerned with their work or their studies. That was his only channel of communication, and he did not know how to talk about anything else with them. He looked on enviously at the relationship Regina had with them and knew there was something: a sharing, a tenderness, which he had never spent time creating. He felt that his sons saw him as an academic tutor rather than a father. It was not to be wondered at, as he had always behaved like one. This was the relationship he had offered them, and Serafín was very aware of this.

We worked on beliefs, values, "what fors". Setting small goals to help him reach a life he would feel more in tune with.

He learnt to say no at work, to set a deadline for finishing, and began investing a lot more time in Regina, as his sons were already living away from home. He had always worked all day; he even had supper at work and still went on working for a couple of hours at home. Conferences, meetings, trips, classes and responsibilities. It took a lot of time to do all this well. Besides, Serafín loved and enjoyed every second of his professional activity, from preparing his classes to teaching, even the most bureaucratic aspects of it.

This was some years past. A little while ago we had coffee together. Serafín was happy, he was enjoying the best time of his life with Regina. He told me that his mistake had been none other than starting from a wrong assumption: he had based happiness on professional success and left the rest of his life to develop all by itself. In the last few years he had been able to establish that even by devoting 40% less time and reducing certain responsibilities which did not bring him any special satisfaction, his professional success had barely changed. He went on being successful in his work environment, but now, in addition to that, he enjoyed many other things he had lost touch with till the age of 55.

He told me that spreading his time across many other activities enabled him to get a different perspective on everything, that now he could see what enriched his life in every way. His mind could now turn to visions of walking in the countryside or cooking with his wife, or playing sport. It seemed an interesting thought to me, and I felt very proud of him. How lucky he was that his world had been on the brink of collapsing.

Where is happiness?

Like Serafín, many of the people I work with look for happiness in the wrong places. Serafín spent many years looking for it in his professional success, whereas others look for it in possessing, in economic wealth. Others think happiness consists of having a significant other, or in the fact that their other half loves them.

For Serafín the only way to happiness was prestige, being known in the university world, publishing scientific articles, his own prominence. But it does not matter whether you are well-known or not, because if you live the life you really want, if you are happy, it does not matter whether people know you or not. And if you have prestige, or money, and you are not happy, it does not matter either.

Balance

More and more studies show that happiness lies in balancing certain very basic things that are fully within the reach of any wallet.

Happiness lies in sharing time with the people you love, with those you like to be with, in exercise and time spent outdoors. But when work and daily chores cloud your vision, those things that bring you so much are the first you give up. You give up being with the people you love, you give up exercise and spending time outdoors. Precisely the things which have been shown to give us most happiness and which in addition do not entail spending money.

That is why the system I advocate, and which I am currently working on more and more, is to focus my efforts on balance instead of on work. When we turn our focus on balance, we leave space in our lives for each of the important things.

Yes, it is true, there may be a deadline for handing in that report, or finishing the marketing plan; perhaps you can employ all your efforts in a precise way for a short period of time. But if there is always something urgent, then the people you love, space in the open air, taking care of your diet or your body ... disappear. Today's time disappears, tomorrow's time disappears, so does the day after tomorrow's, and thus, adding the days together, the time of your life devoted to happiness disappears too.

Do not regret not having seen enough sunsets

Today we went to the Abra de Cosme. Ever since I saw the pictures of this incredible place that a local photographer published on his website (www.fomentografia.com), I decided I had to take a swim in those waters. They did not want to take me there, it was too far. Finally, after insisting, I managed to convince Julio and Kirenia, my brother- and sister-in-law, who are always looking for ways to please me. The advantage of being a part-time sister-in-law is that when we are together, all that remains is love.

The trip there has been complicated. First we had to find some means of transport that would leave us close to it. We went on one of those motorbikes that pull a little cart behind. Of course, my kids were delighted. Then we had to go up a mountain, then down again. This with three small children. My daughter Carmen refused to walk for the whole trip, and we had to carry her all the time. Two hours there and two back.

We crossed a forest without so much as marked paths, which shows how few people go that way. After the exhausting journey I swam in the lagoon all by myself in the turquoise-blue water, with the sound of the waterfalls, among mountains. I think I will remember this day forever.

When I look back, if today were my last day, if I had to recall the best moments of my life consciously, they would probably fit into a single moment. And probably most of them would have a strong connection with nature.

Out of all the years we have lived, out of all the months, weeks, days, hours, minutes and seconds, we can only consciously rescue a few brief moments.

If today were my last day I would probably want to have seen more sunsets, listened to more music, sung more, felt the breeze touching my face, buried my nose in my children's necks more often so as to breathe in their scent of life.

Because if today were my last day I would not waste a moment remembering a single one of my successes. Without a doubt, I would choose to remember those moments when I preferred to live in love, or in nature.

If I could choose certain moments of my life *a la carte* right now, perhaps I would keep any of those times I spent at the beach swimming, feeling the cold water on my skin.

Perhaps I would also pick some early morning, snug in bed under the comforter, being part of the tangle of bodies, elbows and knees we so often wake up in together. Or when my children were babies, any of those moments when they fell asleep at my breast. Or equally I might remember moments laughing with my friends around a table with cake, and coffee for them, tea for me.

It is true that we have to work to make our dreams come true, we cannot just live on sunsets and morning hugs. And I am not saying that it is impossible for economic reasons, but because the human being is much more complex than that, and happiness does not only involve living in contemplation. All those moments have no meaning if there is not a whole personal structure around them to hold them together. Ultimately, they have no meaning if we are not living the life we really want, because if we are not, then we will probably not even be able to enjoy them.

All the same, try to treasure those moments and not forget them, because if today on this hypothetical last day of my life those are what I miss most, then there must be some truth in what I, and all those who ask for one last sunset or one more breath of fresh air on their face, believe in.

Because nature, sunsets, sunrises, starry nights, swimming in the sea or in a river, the sound of a stream, the warmth of a campfire in the country, the whispering of the trees in the forest, make me, at least, feel I am part of life, one more element of something far greater, that I breathe, that I am one with the universe under an immense sky.

From Fomento to Trinidad

Our time in Fomento is over. We will only come by on our last day to say goodbye and pick up our things.

These days I have felt that I have been gently rocked by its people, by Mamma, my mother-in-law. Gently rocked by the whole family, particularly by my brothers-in-law José and Julio and my sister-in-law Kirenia. A time to switch off, to watch my children playing with their cousins for the first time in my life. To see Kirenia and the kids singing: "Roll, roll, bread and cinnamon roll..." With my daughter's crying at night, when I put her to bed and she does not want to sleep because she wants to keep playing with her cousin Julito (Tulito in her baby-talk). For the nights when Milko, my children's brother, tells my son Miguel stories to send him to sleep, while I watch them with all the tenderness a heart can find room for.

I have known Milko since he was only months old, and all these years I have seen him grow and turn into a fantastic young man who fills me with pride. Seeing him now with my children I feel that at last, for the first time, my family is complete. The gap he leaves, the way we miss him, follows us every day he is not with us, and there are many of them. Not having him there is what weighs heaviest on me about living so far away.

I have enjoyed recognizing some of my children's features in the family. Also the parties. And the game of dominoes, which brings that Cuban mischievousness I love to the table.

I love Christmas in Fomento, particularly because it is shorter, because it is not cold, and because what matters is friendship, family and love, not what you eat or give away. Fortunately the Christmas consumerism of our world has not yet arrived there, or at least not in my circle, and that means I can enjoy the season with no headaches.

On December 30th we went to Agabama for lunch with Francis and his family. My son tried passion fruit, and everyone's children were playing together well into the night, in total freedom in Francis' parents house beside the river Agabama. There we cooked food from all over the place, and they lent me their new frying pans to make a Mallorcan *sauté* with a Caribbean touch.

I love Agabama, its floating bridge and its waterfalls.

We celebrated the 31st with family and neighbors. In Cuba the New Year's Eve holiday begins early in the morning, in the kitchen of every home, where the stoves are lit to prepare traditional dishes. Meanwhile the neighbors go from house to house, bottle of rum in hand, to drink toasts with friends. True, some of them fail to make it to dinner, a side effect of the warmth of love together with rum.

And then we spend New Year's Day with Yenellys's parents. We are always welcome at Zobaida and Juan Miguel's, and they cook for everybody there. That day there were a lot of us: us and our children, their children, their grandchildren, and a bunch of friends. There was plenty for everyone, yucca, rice, pork, *chicharritas*, crème caramel and fruit juices. We spent the day eating, chatting, finding each other, remembering, laughing, reminiscing. All the while my son steals Zobaida's freshly-made *chicharritas*. You always eat too little in Zobaida's opinion, and she tempts you with all kinds of treats. My husband Jorge meets old friends again, like José, who now lives in Vietnam and is here on vacation too. I miss the grandmother, Calixta, who left us a few years ago. One of those universal grandmothers, as I would like to be myself when I am old, and whom I know I will never be. She always saved my husband the bottom part of the rice, which is slightly burnt and tastes so good, and warned him when she thought I was not listening that I was a very nice girl and for heaven's sake, he should behave well with me.

Fomento and its people… here I feel at home, in this area of intense greens and streams which is as yet undiscovered by tourists. A wild place where the most essential Cuba endures. That rich soil where everything grows, where everything in the forest is edible.

We are now heading to Trinidad. I spoke of the city before; it is perhaps the prettiest city in Cuba, and for me one of the most special places in the world. It is one of the best preserved colonial cities of the Americas and a World Heritage Site. The cobbled streets have ruined more than one pair of high heels, some of mine among them. They say nobody really knows where those cobbles came from, because they are not from the area. Some even suggest they were brought from Africa as ballast in the over-laden slave ships.

Its colonial houses, many of which are a hundred years old, are magical; here you feel you are just one more of the hundreds who have slept under their roofs. And that after you many others too will sleep, perhaps in the course of the next few centuries too. In one of those houses, Teresa and Rodolfo's, my favorite place to stay in Trinidad, my son Miguel was conceived. Isabel, Teresa's daughter-in-law (and probably the best cook in all Trinidad) and I always joke about it.

While I was hoping to get pregnant with Miguel, who made us wait a few months, Isabel Bécker, "La Profunda" (the Deep One), known in all Cuba as part of the Nueva Trova Cubana, was helping me with her prayers. Every time I arrive in Trinidad I go to see her. I am enormously privileged in that she considers Jorge a "deep one" too, and that she has sung for us alone with her guitar, which I seem to remember was a gift from Pablo Milanés. To sit in her room right beside La Casa de La Trova in those old rocking chairs while she sings just for Jorge and me with her husky voice, with its touch of Chavela Vargas, makes the tears well up in my eyes every time. My emotions never get used to the magic of that little room, full of stories past and stories to come. That room full of photographs of an entire life, her life, mingled with the songs and the faces of legendary international singers and musicians.

To sit in the doorway with her and her stick while she shares her wisdom with me is one of the privileges life has given me.

From her room I witness the passing of time, and also the passing of my own time. I remember when she used to help me so that *Yemayá*, the goddess of fertility, would visit me. And now I see myself here, with my children already walking on their own, messing around in her things and making me nervous, playing with the window-grilles of her house.

Everything is different in Trinidad. Partying, the buzz, the restaurants which fill the streets, the tourists, the taxis, the drums, the Afro-Cuban music, salsa, maracas, *candonga* and all the other extras have banished silence for me. They have already installed wifi here. Although just once, and thanks to a hurricane, many years ago, I also knew a Trinidad that was silent...and dark.

Let us go on...

chapter five

ESSENTIALLY LOVE

"If nothing saves us from death,
at least let love save us from life."

Pablo Neruda

After years of research and analysis, the psychiatrist and writer Elizabeth Kubler-Ross declares that people's greatest need has always been love. According to the doctor, we come into this world to heal one another's souls. We come to this world with unfinished business from other lives, where instead of truly living, we simply existed.

The way to heal our souls is through unconditional love, which according to her is the only way to find peace and happiness in this world. I do not know whether we arrive as souls with unfinished business, but I totally agree that unconditional love is one of the best ways of finding happiness, and probably the most powerful weapon that exists.

It even disarms the most aggressive people, who deep down are the ones who most need love. Love is capable of healing not only incomplete souls, but also the world.

In 1993 John Hagelin, one of the gurus of transcendental meditation, was in charge of the Collective Practice of the Transcendental Meditation program, with whose aid violent crimes decreased by more than 20% in Washington DC. A large group of people came together to meditate, influencing the collective emotional state of the whole city.

In the early '80s Hagelin worked as a psychiatrist in one of the hospitals with the most dangerous criminal patients. It is claimed that without ever seeing his patients, using only their files and the application of Ho'oponopono techniques, he managed to heal them, reducing staff absenteeism in the process, and over time even managed to have that particular ward closed down. Since then the practice of meditation in schools has been proven to reduce violence and improve both attendance rates and student efficiency.

QUALITY
time

*"She gave me her hand and nothing more was
needed. It was enough to feel that I was welcome.
More than kissing her, more than going to bed
together, more than anything else, she gave me
her hand and that was love."*

Mario Benedetti (The truce)

That is why, because there is a collective conscience, it is important to be
at peace with oneself. Not only for one's own good, but for the influence
this might have on others. From the people closest to us, such as our
workmates or our family, to others far away.

Some will find the peace, serenity and acceptance which will improve
their world in meditation, others will do so through completely different
practices. Here in Cuba, surrounded by artists, I see each of them finding
peace and serenity in the things they do. Yram editing videos; Yenellys
showing her most creative side everywhere: Photoshop, cooking or
drawing; Francis among his paintbrushes, Damarys sewing and Pedro
deep-sea diving. Each one with their own thing or their particular mixture
of things.

One of the things which have always caught my attention in Cuba is the
amount of time available. Time probably passes differently in every place
in the world, days do not last twenty-four hours everywhere. I remember
days going by very quickly in Madrid. They slipped between transport,

traffic jams and work. In Mallorca time may pass a little more slowly, in winter more than in the summer.

But in Cuba time goes by wonderfully slowly. It is true that life has its own element of complication, but people have time to be with their family, to devote themselves to their enthusiasms and to live more slowly.

Perhaps that is why they do not need to resort as we do to yoga or meditation, because their environment already allows them to live a life at peace with themselves, in complete and absolute synchrony with the most glorious nature.

Hence my wish to spend a part of the year here, so that the time I live can go by more slowly, surrounded by these wonderful people and this rich soil.

SILENCE
that burns the soul

*"She prayed to God to have at least a moment
so that he would not leave without knowing
without any doubt that she had loved him above
all doubts either of them had ever had, and felt
an irresistible urge to start all over again with
him from the beginning so as to tell each other
everything they had left unspoken, and do well
whatever they might have done badly in the past.
But she had to surrender before the intransigence
of death."*

**Gabriel García Márquez
(Love in the Time of Cholera)**

I do not believe there is a single book I have written up to now in which I do not talk about saying what we feel. Perhaps because for some time I was so afraid to express how I felt to others, that when I discovered that if I did, not only did the world not collapse, but that it was even better, it came as a pleasant surprise.

A popular saying goes: *you're the owner of what you keep quiet about and the slave of what you say.* This may be true of rumors, but as far as feelings are concerned it could not be more wrong.

I wish I'd had the courage to express my feelings

According to Bronnie Ware this is another *I wish* people utter before their last breath. I wish I had said what I felt.

Many people are afraid to express what they feel. Emotions are penalized from childhood: "don't cry", "what'll people think if they see you cry?". But not only crying; happiness and joy are also penalized in childhood: "can't you just stay still and behave?", "don't make so much noise". Then comes adolescence, when it seems the only love is the one which is returned, and that it is a sin to feel anything for someone who feels nothing for you. So you do not say what you feel until you are completely sure that your feelings are returned. Otherwise you would appear vulnerable, and you are strong. There is no other option.

I have found this to be true over and over again, not only with myself but with my clients. When they have the courage to say what they feel, above all after keeping it hidden for long periods of time, they feel a great relief, even when the response is not the one they had hoped for.

But the "fear" of saying what we feel is found not only within the ecosystems of relationships but within families. Parents who are unable to say "I love you" to their children, or children to their parents. Some have never said it, they are not used to saying it, they do not know how to say it, nobody taught them how to. Others knew how to say it when their children were small, or if they did not know how to say it at least they knew how to show it, but then their children grew up, turned first into teenagers and then into adults, and those parents who drooled over their children when they were little never learnt another way of communicating.

And they feel it, deep down in their hearts, but the problem with all the unsaid "I love yous" is that they burn the soul.

A short while ago I saw an image on social media of a girl whispering in her grandfather's ear: "Grandpa, *if I'd known you were leaving* I'd have told you I love you." And when I saw it I was furious (yes, it happens to me sometimes, by myself in my office, when I read nonsense like that). What do you mean, if I'd known you were leaving? Why? Did you have to know he was leaving? Did your grandfather not deserve to hear you say *I love you* without having to die so that you would finally tell him? What kind of world is this? What point have we reached when someone writes something like this on social media and everybody says "ooooh" and nobody gets furious the way I do?

If you search on the Internet you will find thousands of moving letters of people saying farewell to someone who has already died. They did not have the courage to say those words to the person who was beside them. They were ashamed, they could not, and then they publish it on the internet to let the whole world know, or to let it float away on the wind. Grandchildren, children, even parents, regret the hugs they never gave, or the *I love yous* they never said.

And now let me invite you to think: who did you love most who is no longer in your life? A grandfather perhaps, or a parent, or a friend? If you had a moment, ten seconds, to be with that person once again, what would you do? What would you say? Think, think about it just for a few seconds. I'll wait for you...

...

...

...

Don't tell me, I think I know. Could it be a hug, a kiss, and/or an *I love you?* Well then, what are you waiting for? Now that he/she is near, give them to that person, and in a moment, when you open your eyes again, get up and look around. You will die, your whole family will die, your friends will die, your children will die, your significant other will die. You will all die. If, like the girl and her grandfather, you need to know that they are going to leave before you can say "I love you": well, I am telling you now. They will all go. So will you. Now you cannot say "if I had known", now you do know. You have no excuse. Say it now.

And if you still do not believe me, if you still think you have all the time in the world ahead of you, even if you believe you do, you will never pass by here again, at this precise moment. Now it is here, and this same moment it has gone.

How many "I wish I'd said I love yous" do you have around you? How many "I love yous" burn your soul and die before they cross your lips?

"Hail life!"... Is nobody answering?

And what now of all my yesterdays?
My years have been gnawed away by Fate;
My hours, obscured by my folly.
With never a sign of How or Whither,
Health and age alike have fled!
Life's gone, yet what I've lived is present,
And calamities stalk close at my feet.
Yesterday's past, tomorrow not yet here;
Today is slipping away. I am
A was, a will be, and a weary am.
Today, tomorrow and yesterday,
I unite diapers and shroud, and remain
A sequence, all present, of departed ones

Quevedo, Spanish Parnassus.

THANK YOU
is a magic word

**"It is not joy that makes us grateful; it is
gratitude that makes us joyful."**

David Steindl-Rast

At the moment my daughter is three. A long, long time ago, when she
must have been a year and a half or two, we went up to the roof terrace
one day to hang up the laundry. I have no idea why, but we stopped on
the last step and talked for a while. She in her baby talk, and as for me I
do not even remember what I told her or sang to her. Now every time we
go up there she wants us to sit down on that last step and talk as we did
that time. Something I attached no importance to was a blast for her, and
it has become ingrained in her memory. Perhaps if she were asked what
she is grateful for about the time she spent with me or what moment she
remembers, she would say it was the day on the step.

The letters we find on the internet regretting what they did not say to
their dead, or those my clients write after the departure of loved ones,
are filled with gratitude. And not one of them says "Thank you, dad,
for buying me a car". The gratitude is for time, for glances, for smiles,
for stories, for tales, for things learned. People are grateful to them for
teaching them to be strong, for having been proud of them, for the time
they spent reading together, for teaching them how to ride a bike or walk
on stilts. The shared laughter, those vacations, having felt taken care of
when they took you up to bed already asleep, having taught you about

life, the advice given, the concern for you...

The silenced gratitude burns just the same as the unsaid "I love yous". Someone leaves and you never said "thank you", looking into their eyes with love, with time to digest it.

But what happens with the gratitude that is spoken aloud? "Thank you" is a magic word, and if not, go ahead and try it.

Exercise 1: I invite you to look around you. Look for someone, a friend, a relative, a work colleague, think for a second what that person brings to your life. If that person brings you nothing it does not matter, go on to the next one, until you find someone. Go and say thank you for whatever it is they offer you in your life. If you can, hold their hands while you say it, look into their eyes and thank them, slowly, enjoying every word. Watch how you feel, or how the expression of the person changes when you say thank you. When you finish, wait to see what happens, or give them a hug.

Exercise 2: Look for someone really important in your life and imagine that person has disappeared from your life forever. Even let yourself feel the pain of the loss. Now that you still have time, what do you want to tell them? What would you regret not having told them if you were never going to see them again? Go and tell them, following the same procedure as before.

Exercise 3: I invite you to look around you once more, but this time at the things you have in your life. Perhaps a roof, the breeze caressing your face, a plate of food, a comfortable bed, a family, someone who loves you, a job, some socks, having met someone, being alive, the coffee you had this morning, company. When you have chosen - one or several of these things - feel the gratitude for what you have in your life. Feel it and watch the feeling in your body: how does gratitude show itself in you?

Exercise 4: How about a notebook with the things you are thankful for? Take a notebook and write down in it every day the things to be thankful for on that particular day. Surely even in the worst-case scenario there will always be something to feel grateful for. In my case, on the worst days, at the very least I always find something new I have learnt.

How many times are we grateful for everything we have? Being able to breathe, sleeping in a bed, our children's smiles, even their tears; our health, the food we enjoy, being able to sleep under a roof, the warmth of our home... Why do our most precious treasures sometimes have to be suddenly threatened to make us appreciate them?

Exercise 5: Make a small altar in your home. It can be as simple as a candle and two pebbles, or a statuette, or one of those little fountains with water. I do not know, whatever you want that symbolizes life, or whatever you want that is special for you. Find a significant moment of the day. For some it is the first hour in the morning, for others it is night. Play music if you need to and dedicate a minute, a single minute of the day, to feeling grateful for everything you have in your life.

Live in love

Living gratitude in our lives makes our focus center itself on the good things that surround us, and on the way our capacity for love can multiply still further. And apart from that, we can release those words into the wind which if they remain trapped inside us, in time will burn.

It is true that life sometimes sets us hard tests, but even then there is always something to be learnt from them, as well as something to be thankful for.

Along our way we also find people who do not make things easy for us. But nobody is bad of their own volition. Evil is the product of our past life, of our pain, of our frustration, or perhaps of a childhood in which lack of love stopped us learning. But deep down inside us, each of us has the capacity for love. The true love, the unconditional kind, the kind that listens without judging and without asking for anything in return. I learnt to put myself in another person's shoes a long time ago, to put myself in their skin: in their house, with their body, with their parents, with the same things happening to me as to the other person. And I think: "if I had lived all that, how would I act?" It is from that moment, when you learn to empathize, that forgiveness and understanding come: even though you may not want that person in your life, at least you can understand them.

WHOEVER
walks beside us...

*"You have your way. I have my way. As for the
right way, the correct way and the only way, it
does not exist."*

Friedrich Nietzsche

We are what we are because of every one of the people whose paths we
have crossed in our lives. Because of those who have made us laugh, those
who have made us cry, the ones we have loved, or the ones we have hated.

But it is unlikely that someone will go with us forever. If things come out
as expected, most probably your parents will go before you, your children
will come when you are an adult and they will die after you. You will gain
friends through your life, at school, high school, at college, in different
jobs, in your neighborhood or among your partners' friends.

If you have children they will grow up and as is normal, they will leave to
make their own life. Some might remain nearby, others will fly far away.

And people will come and go in your life, and you will be glad to see
someone you have not seen in a long time, and you will feel sorry to say
goodbye to the people you love, and you will miss them. Some you will
see once a year, at Christmas, or at village festivities; with others the gaps
in time may go on lengthening until they disappear forever.

My friend José Colomar told me long ago that he thought friends were those who walked by your side. But those who did at that precise moment in your life, knowing that perhaps they would not be the ones walking with you next month, or next year. When he said that, his belief gave me great peace, because all my different moves had left me unsettled, having friends scattered all over and unable to be everywhere I would have needed to be.

Since then, instead of seeing people as "un-moveable" in my life, instead of having friends and lovers and loving them with the immaturity of a teenager who thinks everything in her life is going to be "forever", I open the doors of my house to whoever is there at that moment, so that they may come in as often as they want and then leave when their path does not coincide with mine. And so that they can come back whenever they want to.

The perfectly imperfect relationship

We were just two strangers and ten years have
gone by already...
Since we've been together...
my heaven's that of your mouth and at five
degrees below zero my clothes still get in the way
– Melendi (Since we've been together)

I look at Jorge, my husband. He is in the street keeping an eye on the children while he chats with the neighbors. I love him, I do not love him the same way as when I met him, or when I got married, or when we had Miguel, or when we had Carmen. I think that in these last ten years I have invented at least 3,650 ways of loving him.

We always believe that relationships are forever, but relationships also end. Some end with death. Others at any moment. But the worst are the ones which having reached their end, fail to finish. Those we put up with year after year on a basis of routine, of habit, of being too lazy to face up to just how difficult it is to end a relationship.

But I still choose to be with him because I keep getting back much more than I give, because I love him, I desire him, because I laugh, because I know he loves me, because he is simply there. He has been a good companion, and still is one. I often tell him that I love him, but I wonder what would change if I were aware of the end, that our time together is finite? That perhaps tomorrow he will not love me? That he will not want me to go on being his companion?

I like to feel that our time is finite as I look at him. I imagine I only have one day, a few hours or this week left to be with him, and I am able to feel even more love. Love for all we have been through together, gratitude for our children, and I suddenly forget all those things I do not like about him. I forget his grumbling when he gets up in the morning and it is cold, or his habit of listening to rock music at full blast while he hammers away in the garage. I forget everything that bothers me and only remember what I like, because the infinite love which comes with awareness of the finite makes me focus on what is really important.

I like loving him like this, without attachment, without possessiveness, knowing he is not mine and that he is only here now, at this moment, because he is walking beside me. Knowing we are both free to do whatever we want with our lives, and that if today we are together it is because we both decided to be.

I get up and hug him hard; he is not surprised, he thinks it is a regular hug, one of those you give unconsciously, without imagining how much love I feel in my heart right now. He simply returns the gesture, gently stroking my arm while he goes on watching the children and waving at the people passing by in the street.

Being good parents

One of the things Ric Elias thought about after he was saved from death on the flight that came down on the Hudson River was that from that moment on he wanted to be a good father. There is nothing more fleeting than our children. Those creatures born of your body, who manage to make you feel an infinite love you never ever imagined you would reach.

Those who make us stronger than ever, who bring out the best in us, the worst, your sweetest words, your yelling. They are fleeting indeed, because they change day by day before our eyes and we have barely a moment to love them as they are now. I look at Miguel and Carmen and have to make an effort to remember when they were babies, because now I can only see them as they are today. And they will never be as they are at this moment, it will never be the Christmas when Miguel was five or Carmen three, because they change from day to day.

If I could take a walk through the past, I would go back to the first time I held Miguel in my arms; the first time we came into our home with him in our arms, in the attic apartment in Madrid; to those walks through the Retiro Park when he was a baby. Or else to the day he took his first step, or to that morning, when I was already pregnant with Carmen, when I slept with him in my bed. Or I would go back to the day when I walked out of the hospital, the one in the Ramblas, with Carmen in my arms and tears of gratitude for being able to leave the hospital with my daughter alive after a difficult c-section. I would go back to those evenings with her on the sofa, to her gurgles while I folded clothes.

But those are not my children now, I can no longer walk through those days, that time has passed, and I knew it. I always knew it, I always knew it was fleeting, which was why I tried to absorb every moment. But now I sometimes forget this because they need another kind of attention which does not come as easily to me as when they were babies.

But this time, the one now, is also fleeting, and sometimes I am so tired I do not even remember that this moment too will pass, and that it will probably be the one they remember. Like Carmen's step.

They will not remember everything, they will only remember some things, but I do not know what moment they will choose to remember, which mother out of all the ones I am will remain in their memory. Could it be the one who tells them bedtime stories? Or the one who scolds them when she finds all their toys scattered on the floor? The one who blows soap bubbles with them in the tub or the one that says she has no time to play because she has work to do, or else because she does not feel like it? Because I am all those mothers, but they will only remember one, the one they choose to remember out of all of the ones I am.

If today were my last day I would choose to spend all the time with them and I would do everything they wanted. That would make me happy, because seeing them happy, absorbing all their presence so as to take it far away with me, is what I would choose to do on the last day of my life. And yet, believing I have infinite days to come by their side, here I am writing instead of playing with them, looking at them and getting to know them better.

Because even if my life does not come to an end, most likely in a few years they will no longer want to play with me, or sleep with me. Time with my children is more finite than any other time because they are different every day.

If my life ends I would like to leave them my message, and if I do not spend time with them I will not be able to do it. I want them to know, to have it etched with fire in their souls, that they can have the life they want, that they should never give up, that they should live lives well lived, that they should follow their dreams, that they are magical, that they are capable of achieving anything they set out to do, that they deserve it, that they are unique, special, that I love them and that they are the best thing in my life. And this is only etched with fire if you take it on yourself to say it often, to show them much more often than that, and to make them feel it from infancy. And for that you need time. Like good stews, this can only be managed over a slow fire.

I wish I'd stayed longer with my mother

"When my father died, I was living in another city. I was working a lot, I had a new partner and small children. At that time I was recently separated and I didn't want to make my children suffer economically, so I worked all the hours I could so as to make money.

"I was the only one who could go to my father's funeral. Getting us all there at that time would have been a massive operation, on the lines of D-Day in Normandy.

"My siblings went too, but they lived away from home as well, and they left straight away. I stayed two more days so as to help with the paperwork and

anything my mother might need help with. She asked me to stay a few days longer, but I felt I had to take care of my children and my work and the whole new life I was creating.

"I said no. At that moment, being young, I wasn't aware of how massive her loss had been. She was a great mother, caring towards all of us, always alert to whatever was needed. My father on the other hand was pure energy, joy and vitality. With his death it wasn't just her other half and the father of her children who was gone but everything my father represented in her life. After so many years of marriage, when you lose a spouse it's not just that person you lose, it's everything he was in your life, and my father when he left took that away too.

"Now that I'm older, getting close to the age when she lost my father, I feel she must've felt very lonely. After raising her children, striving in every way, looking after my father...two days later she was left all alone in a city that wasn't even her hometown.

"If I could choose just one day to go back to, that's the one I'd choose. And that day I wouldn't let my everyday responsibilities separate me from my mother's life. I'd stay with her a few days longer, helping her to cross that threshold, making things easier for her so that she could enter this new stage in her life in a stronger state, feeling protected by her daughter and with love all around her."

MJM, 64 years old.

Keeping close to your friends

This is the fourth of Bronnie Ware's *I wishes*: "I wish I'd stayed in touch with my friends."

All through my life I have always been surrounded by very good friends, I have no reason to complain. But as I said a moment ago, it is not always the same ones who have stayed at my side. It has cost me a lot to accept that this happens, but it has. I have always stayed in touch with many of them, but living in so many cities has made me feel as if my heart were divided, and that I follow what many of them are doing through social media and via long-distance conversations.

I have become estranged from some of them for reasons of geography, from others through circumstances of life, or because of having too much work, or because of having children. As in break-ups, there are some friends you lose when you have children, when you no longer feel like going out for a drink, when you would rather stay home rocking your children to sleep instead of going out for dinner. Then, as time goes by, you stop being a part of those friends' lives.

Because friendship is created out of many moments, and when many moments are no longer being shared, friendship turns into something different. But there is still love in the dregs of the glass, that feeling when you talk to them again that the time you have been apart has meant nothing. For me that is the love which belongs to real friendship.

I have decided to distance myself from other friends, from other people, because it was not a balanced relationship, or perhaps simply because I was better off without them. I remember some of those moments as painful, but wise. Sometimes when something is not fulfilling, the best thing is to leave it behind.

Others I have simply lost along the way, and when I meet them, when I sit down with them, I feel as if we were strangers, as if we had never shared a space in our lives, as if the people in front of me were not the same ones who were with me in the past. It may be me who is not the same. Or most likely a bit of both: we have both evolved in different directions and neither the other person nor I are the same as we were when we were friends.

A friend is the person who walks beside you. The one who is there to share your joys in the present moment, and to pick up your pieces when life gives you one of those hammer-blows it has a habit of delivering: so that you can have the opportunity to be a little wiser, so that you can reinvent yourself once again.

Beyond friendship

These days we have spent in Trinidad I have been able to see how terrible the taxi system has become. The change is really noticeable, a Trinidad which is flourishing, but this has made the taxis conspicuous by their absence, has made them terribly expensive and meant that getting from one place to another in this city (and in Cuba in general) has become something akin to Mission Impossible.

Yram and Yenellys's house is a long way from the center. Walking, with two small children, it stretches out a bit, but as we have not seen each other for some time and the children play with other kids in the property, sometimes we stay well into the evening, until after dinner. I love to sit with Yenellys and talk to her while she cooks and cleans. From her window you see the horizon and the sunset, and even sometimes a glimpse of the sea. The cool coming in through the door is very pleasant. Her kitchen top is made of white tiles, and she likes to keep it immaculate. I love to watch her clean it over and over, knowing that the kitchen top is like her heart: white, simple, clean, with each love in its proper place.

I have always said that if one day I become a millionaire, I will hire Yenellys to be my neighbor. The one you tell your woes to when you come home tired, the one who lends you the cup of salt, or the one you can ask to watch your children while you take a bath. When I tell her, she turns thoughtful and then tells me that perhaps I ought to start charging my current neighbors. That way I could earn some extra income.

The hours go by as we talk about all we had building up to say over these four years, and when we have to go back to the house where we are staying it is impossible to find a taxi. After trying and failing, Yram picks up the phone and calls Modesto, who arrives with his car in less than five minutes. Modesto is Pedro's son.

I have a good nose for feelings, and I detect something special, different, between Yram and Modesto.

Pedro has been a friend of Yram's his whole life, since they were children. Both of them come from a village called Manicaragua, but both live now in Trinidad with their families.

Pedro always takes me deep-sea diving in Cuba. He is the only person in the world I do it with because I trust him completely, he makes me feel safe. Besides, he makes me laugh a lot. He takes me to incredible places and at those moments I feel I am flowing with the current of life. When I go to Cuba I love to see him and feel, as with the others, that it is as though time has stood still.

Modesto has picked us up for several evenings now and he refuses any payment, nor will he accept any gift from us. We try to pay him something for his trouble and he throws the money out the window of his car and drives off in a hurry.

We complain to Yram that Modesto will not accept our money, and Yram, who is a cry-baby, like me, goes all soft. I think there is something funny going on here and being a supreme gossip, especially in matters of love, I want to find out what it is.

I get a beer for myself and one for Yram and I corner him by the white kitchen top.

"Why won't Modesto charge us anything? Why do you love each other so much? What's happened here? Either you tell me or I'll bring out the bottle of rum to loosen your tongue. And you know I mean what I say, and when it's a question of rum I'm as hard as nails."

In the end he tells me in tears, his to begin with, mine and his soon after. He breathes in through one nostril and out the other to try not to cry every couple of words, just as he taught my son to do when you cannot hold back the tears. Yram is a wise man who has come to this world to work magic with children.

Modesto grew up in the sea, he was almost born with flippers on, and has spent all his life fishing and deep-sea diving with his father, and many times with Yram. Because he feels his usual environment is the water, he has come to believe he is one with the sea and that perhaps he does not need to come back to the surface to breathe. One of those days, deep-sea fishing, he pushed the capacity of his lungs to the limit and had a blackout.

When Yram (who was already at the surface) looked down, he saw Modesto suspended and unconscious, floating half-way up. He went down promptly and brought him up, then as best he could, whatever way he could, drawing strength from where he had none left, with his weights still on, holding Modesto with his own weights on in his arms, he brought him back to life in the middle of the sea.

There were several more losses of consciousness, several more reanimations, leg cramps, exhaustion, throwing up of blood and water, but in the end everything turned out well. And they brought back the fish they had caught that day, although Modesto ended up in hospital.

But after this experience everything would be forever different between them. When you have been so close to losing a friend, the son of a friend, when your friend saves your son, when everything turns out well when it could so easily have been otherwise ... a feeling is born, a different love that probably goes beyond friendship, beyond love, gratitude, solidarity, from "he's my friend's son" to "I don't know how to thank you for being there that day, and for being here today". Beyond many things that cannot be explained in words.

And I repeat again: why can we not enjoy a love like that of Modesto, Yram and Pedro without having to come so close to losing everything? How can we connect with that kind of love they will have forever, and if there are more lives, beyond this one?

Sometimes it is simply a question of stopping, looking, feeling that the present is no more than an instant in time, and then of finding that feeling that exists and which changes everything. Love leads us to generosity, to gratitude, to love at a higher level, because it is far more intense than anything else.

Endless conversations

Francis and my husband Jorge have been friends since their teens. They probably have thirty years of friendship behind them.

When they talk, and even more now as they do not live in the same geographical area and months go by, even on occasion years, without seeing each other, the world ceases to exist. They talk about their people, about gossip, places, music, philosophy, life and death, about how they view the world, about what they have learnt and what they have yet to learn. Any subject is interesting for them, they can deliberate about anything for hours, and they are tireless. I remember one of the times we came to Cuba I went to sleep one night and left them talking outside on the porch. When I got up the next day I found them in the same place still talking, as if only a few minutes had passed.

Francis's wife Damaris and I talk meanwhile, and she constantly regales me with gifts for me or my children, or teaches me her recipes. Her generosity always surprises me, both me and all the people I have recommended to call at their house and who claim that the best thing in Cuba is my friends.

If you watch them from afar, if you pay close attention, you can see how Francis and Jorge's auras mingle to form a single one, how their energies flow and join, because during those moments, when they are talking, they live in their own world: unique, perfect, magical and impenetrable.

I love to see them; their love, their magic, rub off on me, and they earn my respect. I know that as long as they live nothing will separate them, and that they will keep up their conversations every day they can for the rest of their lives. I can imagine them growing old, sitting in the doorway, laughing and talking as they are doing now and as they have been doing for the last thirty years.

I imagine myself watching, enjoying this magic, watching all our children growing and maturing. Melisa, Francis's daughter, will be whatever she wants to be; she is going to start philosophy at college. As for Guille and our own children, who knows what they will become? It is still too soon to tell. I see them coming and going, eating, laughing and sharing with us. Stumbling, un-learning and learning, maturing, growing and finding their own way. I imagine myself feeling they are part of my life, that I am still a part of theirs. How lucky I was that nothing stopped me from taking this trip, that I found them all.

The communion of souls

We all have friends around us whom we love more and with whom we share more things than with some actual relatives. Some of us have relatives we never see. There are even people who have not seen their siblings in years.

Blood is important, but it is by no means everything. There are times when there is a communion of souls which emphasizes that there is something special that goes beyond the affection that grows with daily contact.

This magic, this spark, this *something* sometimes happens over time, but there are other times when it leaps up minutes after meeting someone. It must have happened to you: you start talking to someone new to you and you feel you have known this person your whole life, you feel as if you were in your own home, as if everything were right, as if at that moment you could be more yourself than ever.

According to Brian Weiss, this is the result of those two people being together in another life. For whatever reason, there are people in this world that we cannot allow to escape, people we have to look after so that they stay beside us, family or not.

There may be a geographical distance, as between Francis and Jorge. Perhaps the vital stages are different, the needs different, perhaps in this moment we might not be able to be together, or those people might not be able to walk beside you, but when that magic has occurred there is always a remnant, that richness that person has left you.

It does not matter whether it is always you who calls, even though it is only twice a year; it does not matter if it is only an email, or a call, or a "how are you?" Do not let them get away, do not let yourself end up remembering this person on your death-bed and wondering "Where can she be? I wish I'd called him, I wish I'd stayed in touch."

Even if something upset you. Sometimes friendships break for some specific reason and everything from before that is forgotten, all the time you spent together, all the time there was love.

The secrets to keeping a good consistent circle of people around you to lean on are few. I believe I hold the key, at least my own key. Move away from the people who steal your energy, or who do not let you grow.

And the others, the ones you enjoy, the ones who value you, who accept you, who love you... keep them close, forgive the things that might have upset you, they are usually unimportant things, forget your pride and take the necessary steps to let the magic go on flowing between you. Even though it may be just every once in a blue moon.

And those who are close to you, make them the gift of your time and be thankful for the time they give you. This is one of the best investments you can make in happiness, in a life well lived. Because it seems to me that nobody on their deathbed would say: "I wish I'd spent less time with the people I love".

Never let that *I wish* ever come out of your mouth, never let the monster of Everyday eat up the magic of having a circle of people around you who can supply you with love, laughter and shared moments.

chapter six

AND BEYOND LOVE IS MAGIC

*"It is life,
rather than death,
that has no limits."*

**Gabriel García Márquez
(Love in the Times of Cholera)**

We live on the planet Earth, a planet that goes round and round a star, like other planets in our solar system, which in turn is in a galaxy, one of the thousands of millions of galaxies that exist. On our planet the necessary conditions were there for the appearance of life, which evolved into what we ourselves are. Beings with consciousness, with a soul, who reflect on the future and try to understand their past.

We think and feel, but within us we are made up of a self-regulating system. Our hearts, our breathing, our digestions, work on their own, we do not have to do anything in order to "function". If you have not seen pictures of the inside of the human body, I invite you to look for them. There are fantastic documentaries like *Journey inside the Human Body*. Our inside is awesomely beautiful.

To me, although this may be called science, it seems magical. Is there not magic in all this complexity that allows me to be here and now, existing, as I write these words?

There is still much to discover, thousands of species we still do not know. For example, we have yet to discover four-fifths of Egypt. And of the universe? The truth is that we barely know a thing! And the same is true of the brain, cancer, or the future.

But there is still more than that, there are probably things still to be discovered in areas we have not even found yet, areas we cannot even imagine, which go far beyond what we can conceive. Currently what I consider magic is called science; perhaps one day what is today considered magic will be called science.

We all know there is magic in our lives too, something that goes far beyond thoughts and coincidences. Intuitions, premonitions, wishes coming true that we never thought could come true, thinking about someone we have not seen for a long time and then meeting them. Hans Berger discovered EEG (electroencephalograms) from the evidence that the human brain transmits an electric current. He researched all this on the basis of a telepathic episode with his sister.

For all these things we can find hundreds of explanations in quantum physics, or laws of attraction, which attempt to provide answers. But my brain seizes up when somebody talks of laws referring to something which to me is magic and to which no rules can be applied. For example, the one that says that if what you want to happen to you fails to happen, it is because you are not applying the rules properly. I know great people, people who are optimists, good people, who are delighted with their lives and to whom nevertheless horrible things happen which they cannot explain through any law of attraction. If the law of attraction is real, what I can certainly assure you is that it does not work the same way for everybody.

But there is still something magical in living: something which for me, however much I may have read on the subject, is difficult to explain. When you flow with the universe, are grateful, do good and live love, sometimes wonderful things happen. This does not mean bad things are guaranteed not to happen. Many sad things will go on happening to you. You will still lose loved ones, the car will still keep breaking down, and bills will keep on coming.

When your spirit looks for gratitude, tries to understand, seeks to learn from everything that happens to you, then your gaze is focused on always finding *something* positive in what is happening in your life, whatever the circumstances may be.

YOU CAN ONLY JOIN
the dots by looking back,
not ahead

Wanderer, your footprints
are the road, and nothing more;

Wanderer, there is no road
the road is made by walking.

By walking one makes the road,
and upon glancing behind
one sees the path
that never will be trodden again.

Wanderer, there is no road,
only a ship's wake on the sea.

Antonio Machado (Proverbs and song)

I sometimes feel we have come into this world to learn, as many people preach, and the universe takes it on itself to put the right stones in our path so that we can learn from them. Or perhaps things simply happen, and if we are intelligent enough, or our instinct for survival is great enough, we decide to learn to be happy with whatever luck we have been allotted, and transform it into a process of learning.

Perhaps we have a fate which is already outlined and we overcome the tests which were decided on at our birth, or perhaps we ourselves trace our fate as we go with the stones we find on our path.

What is certainly true is that whatever may be happening, the dots can only be joined by looking back, not ahead. This is one of my favorite reflections from Steve Jobs' speech. Of course he illustrates his explanation with brilliant sayings like: *Sometimes the brick hits you on the head, but that's always for a reason.*

Since the first time I heard the speech, this sentence has always been with me. When I have one of those great moments I remember everything I have had to go through in order to get here, and I realize it would not have been possible if I had not suffered a little. When I have a bad moment I think of what I might learn from what is happening to me, and believe it will lead me somewhere unexpected. I let the brick hit me on the head and I go on walking.

My friend Gemma Martín Sánchez is an expert at seeing things from the other side. When things I do not like happen to me, things I would rather had not happened, or when I feel sad, or cannot find a solution, she is the one I turn to. When I arrive, distressed and in floods of tears, and tell her what is going on, together we find out all the positive aspects of whatever it may be. Never, ever, have we finished our "key" meetings without exclaiming *"Qué suelte!"* (How lucky we are!) And let me explain: we say it with an *l* instead of an *r,* and I cannot even remember why, but we have said it that way for at least the last twenty years, and chanting those words with her like this makes hope spring up in my heart.

No matter how much you try, no matter how much you visualize what you want, no matter how expert you may be in the law of attraction and quantum physics, painful things will happen to you in your life. No matter how much you want it and how well you visualize it, the path to your dreams will never be the one you were expecting. You may well have to walk many paths, turn back, go forward, adjust and readjust your compass in order to get to the place you want to.

But each time you have to go back, each time you have to adjust, you also have the choice between giving up, or saving that learning, that experience, that brick, in your bag, and letting it be one of those dots you decide to join one day.

And whatever happens, you can think that everything is lost, that you will never be able to lift your head up again, or on the other hand you can learn from the experience and extract something positive from it, thinking that the universe, instead of giving us what we ask for, gives us what we need so that we can learn and be able to take the next step.

AND DREAMS
come true

"What is life? A frenzy, an illusion,
A shadow, a delirium, a fiction.
The greatest good's but little, and this life
Is but a dream, and dreams are only dreams."

Pedro Calderón de la Barca
(La Vida es Sueño), trans. Roy Campbell

If I look back to the girl I was, that girl of twenty from a working class family, that little girl who lived in a small village in a small Spanish island, a country with a recently-installed democracy, where everything was still seen in black and white... I cannot believe how many things I have accomplished since then, and how many dreams have come true.

Dreams I never even dared to dream have come true, dreams I was able to dream as I went up the steps of that staircase we were talking about before. And I still dream, and I know many of my dreams will arrive, that they are still to come.

But I can also say that dreams have never arrived when I wanted them to, but a long time later (which is what happens when you are impatient). They have arrived at the right moment, at the moment when I had learnt what was needed to manage them, because I dare say if they had arrived earlier, I would not have known how to do the right thing. No matter how much I might have believed I was ready, that I wanted it there and then, that I needed it at that precise moment, I still had things to learn before I could live my dream in the best possible way.

And neither did any of those dreams come wrapped in the exact kind of wrapping paper I had imagined. Dreams, when they come, are made out of what you really need, which might not be the same as what you had imagined. It might even be better, but still different.

I know that when you manage to dream in such a way that you flow with life and with love, the universe conspires to open those doors that lead you to the place you want. The first act, the most important one of all, is the act of dreaming itself. Giving your imagination wings so that it can alight on the essence of your dreams, on the temperature, the colors, the feelings, the voices, the sounds. Letting it live in your imagination and enjoying having achieved it. A game from which you expect nothing.

I know how it is done, though I do not always manage it, and it has a lot to do with everything we have talked about up till now. A pure heart, a life in peace, gratitude for everything you have, learning from everything that happens to you and working to spread smiles and love everywhere you go.

FOLLOW
your intuition

*"You only see with your heart,
what is essential is invisible to the eyes"*

Antoine de Saint-Exupéry (The Little Prince)

We all have magical episodes in our life. Me in particular. I could give hundreds of examples of them. From having premonitions of something that is about to happen in my life, to intuitions which clearly point out the path to be followed.

I do not always manage to let myself be led by intuition; I have always had this internal dialogue with myself, the result of the cerebral training I was subjected to as a result of living in the era of *don't feel, just think*. Now, more and more often, with each path I choose I have to make an effort to feel instead of think. To decide according to my intuition. Unlearning what I have learnt so as to choose my paths through feelings.

Intuition is not something you listen to, but something you feel; sometimes it lasts just for a moment, it passes in front of your eyes and then hides. If you do not pay attention to it, you miss your chance. Other times, though, it insists over and over again and flutters around you telling you which way to go, wanting you to take its hand.

Intuition only appears when you are at peace with the world, when everything is quiet. At the most unexpected moment, suddenly, those flashes of light appear, and when you stay true to them all doors open before you.

It is like what happens when someone is drowning. Fear is the first reaction, putting all one's physical effort into surviving, moving arms and legs as fast as possible. The result is exhaustion. The second reaction is serenity, trying to save your strength so as to resist as much as possible, letting yourself drift with the current while you look for a way out. In the first reaction there is only space for instinct; in the second reaction you leave space to think, to flow, and of course to allow for intuition.

The same thing happens in life, because if we only live in a space made up of instincts there is no room for intuition. And intuition needs to find a clear path so that it can reach us.

That is why if you are looking for an answer, you have to stop struggling and simply let the currents take you while you find peace again, and hurl the question at the heavens. Do not be afraid if the answer does not come. It never comes straight away. Keep hurling questions and let yourself drift. When intuition finds its way, it will light your way with its brilliance.

Today it should be the end

"We'd been together for three months and we'd just made love. It wasn't ordinary sex, it was one of those times you know are special, when there's this incredible feeling of communion of the spirits on both sides. Everything was silent, souls in peace, bodies resting. The perfect moment for intuition to find you. The silence you need so that you can hear it.

"*I was sitting naked on the bed, with Gilda's head on my knees, hugging my legs. A message crossed my mind for a moment: 'This story should end today', and I had the certainty that this was absolute truth. That this was the best I could do at that moment. Up to that moment everything had been perfect, but to be more perfect still, our story would have to end that day.*

"*I was so absolutely sure my intuition was right that I told Gilda at once, in the tenderest way I could manage. Her eyes began to fill with tears and she implored me desperately: 'No, please, don't, this can't end here, I love you, this is too beautiful, it's forever, don't you realize?'*

"*My heart was overwhelmed, and when sadness came intuition flew away, and though I'd already made my decision, I wanted to please Gilda, I didn't want to see her sad, and I told her not to be sad, that everything would be all right.*

"*This relationship lasted seven years, we both ended up exhausted with fighting to save something that just couldn't last, with our hearts broken. We had to build a new life on top of the ruins of the life we'd shared, and there were a lot of those ruins.*

"*Until now I thought I wouldn't change anything in my life. That all the steps I'd taken had led me to be the person I was, and I was very satisfied with every single one of my decisions. But after you asked me, this moment came into my mind.*"

Alex, 47.

St. Lucia's Pebbles

St Lucia's Pebbles, as they are known in my part of the country, are curiously-shaped pebbles which can be found on the beach. They belong to snails named *Astraea rugosa*, as my friend Juana told me the day I lost a bet with her about the origin of these pebbles. I had always believed they were snail shells which had been eroded out of shape by deep-sea currents.

In Cadiz they are called Zahara's Little Ears, in other places Migraine Stones, and in others St Lucia's Eyes. In many places around the world they have been used to make jewels and beads, and in many cultures they are a synonym of peace, or love, or luck, or happiness. In Mallorca with my mother, with my relatives, with my friends, I have always looked for these little fragments of stone on the beaches. I used to spend hours looking for them when I was little.

I knew nothing about them, just that they were pretty, that they were used to make necklaces or earrings and that they brought me luck. Every time I made a wish and found one, my wish would come true. And if I really, really, *really* wanted something I would go to one of my favorite beaches, Ses Covetes, bury my wish in the sand and look for a pebble that would make sure it would come true. I still do it every once in a while.

Whether because of the pebbles or not, most of the wishes I have made in my life have come true. And as for those that have not, it has been because they were not really the right thing for me, because fate had something even better in store for me. Remember, you can only join the dots by looking back.

The first day I went to Playa Ancón I remember I woke up sad and a little melancholic. Some things about the trip had not come out as I had wanted, and I was feeling a certain nostalgia about things that had happened in the previous few months. I had been in Trinidad for two days, and although I had had a very good time, I felt something was missing.

I thought the beach was wonderful: there was barely a soul around and I had miles of white sand and crystal water at my feet. When I looked down at the sand I saw one of St Lucia's pebbles, bent down to pick it up and suddenly saw another, and another, and another. I had never seen so many together, I did not even have to look for them, there were dozens of them all around even without moving from where I was. I collected some and spent the day on the beach, intending to go back to Trinidad later on. That afternoon there came one of those tropical summer downpours which leave the air clean and the soil smelling of rain. Rain is another of those things that always leave me with a feeling of magic and peace, a feeling that everything is possible.

Because of that, by the time the rain had stopped I had already forgotten about the pebbles and my sadness when I reached the steps at Trinidad, which were packed with people. That evening, for the first time, my gaze met that of Jorge, who would later be the father of my children. Although we are still arguing more than a decade later about which of us wooed the other, we both agree that the first time our eyes met we felt we had come home, as if we had known one another for ever.

And that was what they were like, the days that followed that day and that trip. I met those who have since become part of my life, great teachers who came with the package and who have been with me ever since. They have the power to fill my heart with love.

From that moment on my life would never be the same, because part of me remained anchored forever to Cuba. To the white beaches of Trinidad, to the music that makes hearts sing and the intense green that covers the hills of Fomento; and most of all, the wisdom of its people.

I had never connected St Lucia's pebbles with that day until today, when we spent the day at Playa Ancón: Jorge, our children and Yram. I was picking up pebbles with Miguel and Carmen, who by now can tell them apart, when I suddenly realized. That day, my first day at Playa Ancón, the day I met the man I would make a family with, was the day when I saw more St. Lucia's pebbles than ever before in my life.

It was then that the whole universe and the infinitude of stars that night conspired to open the door for me to a new destiny with the man I had dreamed about on another beach, and who has brought me here today. Who has given me this perfect vacation with our children Miguel and Carmen, which in turn has forced me into three weeks of digital silence, thus allowing me to connect with my intuition and enabling my fingers to produce, almost without my realizing it, the book you are now holding in your hands.

chapter seven

YOU
AND
YOUR
DEATHBED

*"After all,
death is just a symptom that there was life"*

Mario Benedetti

Playing with death is a tool I often use when coaching. The human mind works in a complex way, we are capable of imagining things that do not exist. Often we suffer in the present because of things which we imagined would happen in the future. Perhaps what we imagine fails to happen, but we have already suffered it, and sometimes we live through it over and over again. At other times we also suffer in the present because of things that are not the way we would like, as well as because of things that have happened in the past.

In the present our mind keeps traveling this way and that, and the problem cannot be solved from the level where we have created it; we cannot work on it from the present. We have to change levels. Among many other tools, the deathbed is a place I often visit with my clients.

You yourself on your deathbed are probably the wisest you because that you has nothing to gain or lose any longer. It knows you better than anyone, it has been through everything you have been through. It has lived in your body, the one you have now, in all the bodies you have had, and in all the ones you still have waiting for you. It knows what you want and how to get it. It knows all your possibilities, how special you are, and your most deeply-hidden wishes. You will not find anybody wiser to advise you. It has all the answers you need.

Talking to yourself on your deathbed only takes a few seconds; once you have practice, you connect with this image, with this being, your most essential being, just before it is turned into pure love. With my clients I usually get this being to sit down beside us.

But today, the last day of my three-week vacation which has produced this beautiful book, I am the one who is going to sit down with myself to compose my own letter, so that I never forget how I am feeling today. Because the future is the product of every conversation we have, with each one we generate new possibilities for action, and this conversation with myself is part of my own future.

I invite you to do the same. If your future you wanted to communicate with you, what would it say?

MY LETTER

*But I want you to tell me, love, that it wasn't all
a shipwreck for having believed love was the most
beautiful verb... Tell me...*

Luis Eduardo Aute (Me va la vida en ello)

I'm delighted to be able to communicate with you in these moments when there's no more time left for me in this life. There are no more sunsets, no more hugs, no more forgiveness. Maybe only a few hours, maybe days. I'm not afraid, I'm calm and grateful for everything that's happened, even for what's happening now. I don't know what's waiting for me afterwards, but that doesn't matter. I've lived a life well lived. If it's true that this has been just a single one of the many lives we live, then I may have new opportunities to meet the people I love, Miguel, Carmen, Jorge, my family, or my friends. There's nothing I'd like more.

I hope you believe what I'm going to tell you now, because it all depends on you: whether or not I can feel satisfied today with my experience of life, whether today I can feel I've done everything I came to do, the particular people who are around me today, at this moment. The ones who are here with me and those who have already left, but in a way are still here because they are part of what I am.

It's been intense, it's gone by quickly. I know the things that worry you - remember, I was there too - but I also know you'll learn to live them in some other way. Stop worrying about the uncertainty of what will happen in the future and enjoy what you have, every day. Because in the end you'll always be all right. You know that if things don't turn out the way you want them to, it's always for a reason. Because there's still something for you to learn, or because what the universe has in store for you will be even better than what you expected. Seeds take time to grow, each one at its own pace, just like wishes and dreams. Learn to be patient. Make sure you water your seeds in the present, enjoy doing it. Enjoy the uncertainty of not knowing what's going to happen, because that means you still have life ahead of you. Even be grateful when nothing's happening, because everything that's happened in your life up till now, and everything that will happen from now on, is exactly what has to happen. Don't let your impatience for the future cloud your gratitude for the present.

Every moment in your life is unique, magical, even the one I'm living now, and from each one of them you have many things to enjoy and many things to learn.

Live in love; I know you've learnt this, I remember it, but you can still achieve more, you can still give it that bit extra so as to live each second with that feeling of being in the right place at the right moment.

Enjoy your children; they'll grow up and leave. You'll watch them go with pride, satisfied to see what they've turned into, then you'll go back into your house and get on with your life. You'll always have things to write about and pictures to paint, but you'll miss them a lot. And you'll want to go back to breathe in their childhood and the perfect, unique family you have now.

I know that sometimes you're tired and you miss the freedom of your own skin when you wake up trapped among arms and legs and feet. But you'll miss the peace of hearing them breathing beside you in the middle of the night, knowing everything's in its place, that everything's where it should be. Enjoy watching them grow, each in their own marvelous, unique essence.

Fertilize their way so that they can sow their own wishes in it. And kiss them for me: that great creator and inventor with the huge heart, Miguel, and that sweet, determined, special and magical Carmen. They've been the best thing that's ever happened in my life, and they've never, ever, ceased to surprise me. Probably this is what I most envy you for today, being able to kiss the children they were. Also being able to kiss the parents I had, and whom you still have.

Enjoy them. Enjoy Mom and Dad. Tell Dad from me that I'll always be grateful to him for all he left me: the courage to bear honesty as his flag, his social skills, his love of his work, and most of all for his sense of humor. And to Mom, tell her thank you for giving me her courage, for teaching me to get up every time I fell down and for fighting like a samurai warrior with her sword so that nothing would block the way to my dreams. Even when she did not understand them.

In these moments, in each one of the moments in your life, in all the moments you still have to come, you'll always have what is sufficient and necessary to enjoy a serene, happy life. You've come a long way, crossed barriers of fear, risen above many crises, but there are still many more for you to overcome, and each time they'll be greater.

Never again decide to earn your living through things that don't fulfill you; we already did that and we didn't like it, remember? You'd do better to stay still, or go fishing the way Yram did, rather than go on swimming against the current and using up your strength on the way. Never stop being a friend of Yram and Yenellys: now they eat lobster, and in case the supply runs out, Yram knows how to catch them.

Never again let fear cloud your way, or paralyze you. Seen from here, those fears which in your present seem invincible are just so many made-up ghosts, like the monster that lived under your bed when you were a child. They terrify you at one particular moment, but as time goes by you realize they don't really exist.

Follow your intuition, and never think the dreams you have are too big. They never are. Don't let anybody tell you otherwise, and go on pursuing them. Accept once and for all that you have many interests, a whole heap of them, not just one, and try to live them all. The way will gradually straighten itself out and everything will settle into the right place. Stay calm, you'll find your balance.

Prepare your future so that you can grow old with people you like to talk with. Friends with whom energy also flows, the kind you never cease learning from. When you're older, when you come closer to death, you'll be pleased to have them near you. As for the rest, you've already learnt the most important thing, that friends are people who come and go, but who remain forever. You've learnt to open the door when they come back and then to let them go again, you've taught your sad ego not to stop you being the one who picks up the phone.

Become the person you already are. Accept it, because that's what's brought you to the life you have now. Accept your body and love it, because it will never be as young as it is now. Accept doing many tasks at once, having ten books half-read... because it's from that variety that your successes spring. Accept being thinly-spread when it comes to learning a thousand and one disciplines; knowing a little about everything is what makes you unique and what allows you to live so passionately - even if sometimes it may get you into trouble.

Accept your magic, don't hide it any more, don't go on looking for rationality everywhere. You'll find thousands of things your rational mind will never be able to explain, things you know are there all the same.

Accept it all, from this moment, and be yourself, authentic, with all that entails.

Don't begrudge the time you spend on anything or anybody, and stop stealing time from important things in order to work. Do it the other way around and devote time to your most creative self, to being at home, to enjoying your tea and your silence, to letting the breeze caress your cheeks, to getting wet in the rain, diving in the sea and burying your feet in the sand. Never prostitute your time at the expense of the many-colored woman who lives inside you.

Life has been a beautiful journey, the most special journey. That is how I've lived it, and something greater than intuition tells me you too will do the same. With your eyes wide open and all your senses set on love.

I'm waiting for you here, at the end of the way.

DEAR
reader

Dear Reader:

Thank you so much for giving up this part of your precious time to reading my book.

I would love you to write to me and tell me what you thought of it. You will find me at info@angelacovas.com. I would also appreciate it if you took a moment to rate the book on Amazon and leave a comment.

Your opinion is so important to me! Each review I get thrills me enormously, as it does all the writers I know. We write for you, unknown reader, and your opinion is a way of feeling that you are close.

BIBLIOGRAPHY

Campbell, J. (1949). *The Hero with a Thousand Faces*. Princeton: Princeton University Press.

Gaona, J.M.(2014). *Al otro lado del túnel: El camino hacia la luz en el umbral de la muerte*. Madrid: La Esfera de los Libros.

Kübler-Ross, E. (1997) *The Wheel of Life: A Memoir of Living and Dying*. New York: Simon and Schuster/Scribner.

Ware, B. (2012). *The Top Five Regrets of the Dying: A Life Transformed by the Dearly Departing*. Carlsbad (CA): Hay House.

ACKNOWLEDGMENTS

I would like to thank all the people who have revised and collaborated on this book, enriching it and enriching me too before its publication:

Silvia Díez, the best editor in the world and a mirror to look at myself which always reflects back new realities as seen by her eyes. Thank you for taking the time away from your sleep and your little Silvia in order to make my books into something much better. And thank you to my books, which give me the excuse to share time with one of the people I most love in this world.

Writer Marleny Morrero, for her generosity, her friendship, her vision of the world, and for the final in-depth revision.

Llars El Temple, Magela Sosa (director) and Alejandro Zahinos (emancipation coordinator), for the gift of their crystalline transparency. Also to Carolina Linuesa and Juana Riera.

Jorge, my significant other, the father of my children, my companion and friend. For reading me, for helping me in the search for the source of perfect water, for commenting, philosophizing after meals and sharing that other dimension of life which has led me to write this book.

Luis Vera Sánchez, for wrapping my amateur writer's susceptible soul in his words and giving it oxygen to keep it growing. And mostly for carrying on endless conversations that began in the past and which (if the Singularity University keeps its wits about it) will not need to end with two toothless friends enjoying the fresh air outside the door arguing (agaaaain) about chance and causes, but will continue with all their teeth they had where they started from: having a few beers at the Lamiak more than a decade ago. With Marina of course.

The great sage Jordi Llonch for his friendship and for bringing his "Jordi touch" to this book. The "Jordi touch" is always like the jewel in the crown, or Arguiñano's parsley. Everything he does he makes unique. And his wife, Olga del Val, to whom I am linked by the respect and friendship Jordi grants us by telling us things about each other. Thank you for reading this book.

Maria Angels Perelló Puig, who, honoring her name whispers blessings at the birth of this book. Gràcies de tot cor, confit. And to her mother, Magdalena Puig, a gift of life as a neighbor. I could thank her for many things, such as reading this book before it was published. But above all, in this space, I would like to thank her for giving me Javier Pérez.

Javier: I would like to thank him for the time he gave to reading this book, and all those words of his that leave my heart full and overflowing with gratitude. Thank you for reading the book two or three times so as to enrich it, and for all those conversations which always bring me serenity, so much serenity...

Those great gifts EFIC gives me. Maria Antonia Froilán. She is a true "cheerleader", pretty (and smart) who passed through my life one day, and after taking a second look I decided to keep her. Thank you for what you have brought me, and for always bringing me your light. Carmen Enseñat, for her courage, her honesty, and for linking her path with mine, both in the words of this book and in our lives. Neus Mateu, for her light, her radiance, her honesty, her transparency, and for always putting my books in the best bookshop in Mallorca: Es Ranconet. Silvia De La Colina, for letting me use her story and for the laughs we had that day.

And of course Juanjo Martín for letting me use his story and for lending me his eyes so as to see myself.

Maria Jesús Lope, a sage of life, although her opinion will remain a secret until the book is published. You will find a sentence or two of yours scattered through the book from one of those long morning telephone conversations.

Victor Fernández, CEO of Mansion Games, a great guy, knight in shining armor who goes into battle displaying his values and defending them with the sword in pursuit of a dream. A pleasure working with you.

Rosa Melisa Rodríguez, for dedicating a night to reading my book at a sitting. Nothing could give more meaning to my work than knowing that you devoted a whole night of your young life to reading me. You see yourself in my words and I see myself in yours. Thank you.

And thanks also to all those who added their little grain of sand: Juana Porcel, Juanjo Martín, Mar Gallardo, Rafael Llobet and Alberto Tarriño.

And to Jandi Sueiras, not so much an intern as a human library, for bringing his knowledge of ancient cultures and for letting me drive him crazy for three months. Three damn months, for goodness' sake!

This book has a little of each and every one of you in it. Thank you for dedicating this precious time from your lives to helping me be a little better.